...nder guide

Glasgow,
the Clyde Valley,
Ayrshire *and* Arran

WALKS

Compiled by
Brian Conduit

JARROLD

Ordnance Survey

Acknowledgements
My thanks for the valuable advice and numerous useful
leaflets that I obtained from the various tourist information
centres throughout the area.

Text: Brian Conduit
Photography: Brian Conduit
Editor: Sarah Letts
Designers: Brian Skinner, Doug Whitworth
Mapping: Heather Pearson, Tina Shaw

Series Consultant: Brian Conduit

© Jarrold Publishing and Ordnance Survey 1999
Maps © Crown copyright 1999. The mapping in this guide is
based upon Ordnance Survey ® Pathfinder ®, Outdoor
Leisure ™, Explorer ™ and Travelmaster ® mapping.
Ordnance Survey, Pathfinder and Travelmaster are registered
trade marks and Outdoor Leisure and Explorer are trade
marks of Ordnance Survey, the National Mapping Agency of
Great Britain.

Jarrold Publishing   ISBN 0-7117-1054-6

First published 1999
by Jarrold Publishing and Ordnance Surve

Printed in Great Britain
by Jarrold Book Printing, Thetford, Norfolk 1/99

Jarrold Publishing,
Whitefriars, Norwich NR3 1TR
Ordnance Survey,
Romsey Road, Southampton SO16 4GU

Front cover: Dunure Castle, Ayrshire
Previous page: Lochranza Castle, Arran

Contents

Short, easy walks

Walks of modest
length, likely to
involve some
modest uphill
walking

More challenging
walks which may
be longer and/or
over more rugged
terrain, often with
some stiff climbs

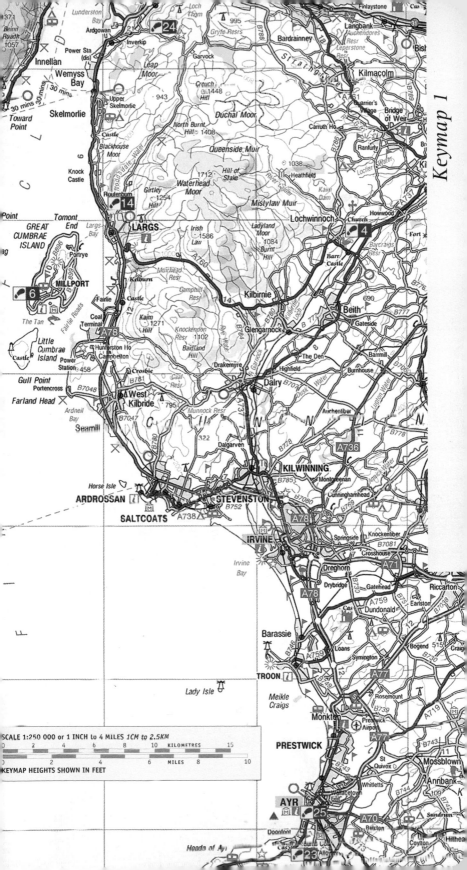

Keymap 1

SCALE 1:250 000 or 1 INCH to 4 MILES *1CM to 2.5KM*

KILOMETRES 15

MILES 10

KEYMAP HEIGHTS SHOWN IN FEET

Keymap 2

SCALE 1:250 000 or 1 INCH to 4 MILES *1CM to 2.5KM*

KILOMETRES

MILES

KEYMAP HEIGHTS SHOWN IN FEET

Keymap 2

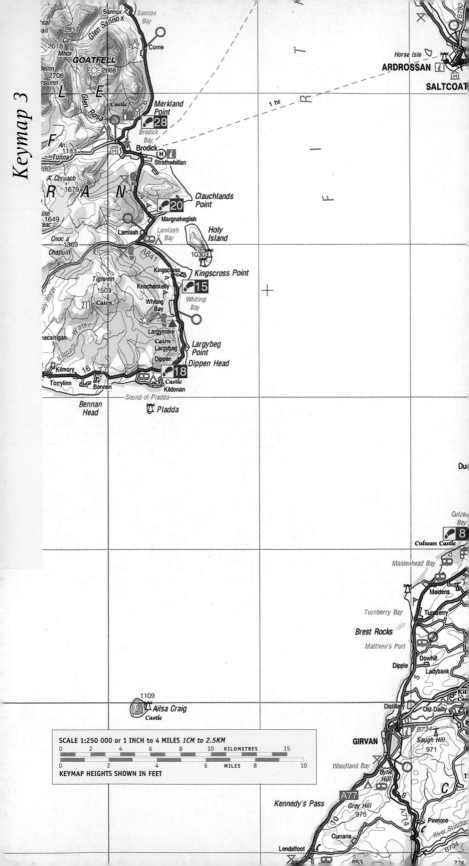

Keymap 3

SCALE 1:250 000 or 1 INCH to 4 MILES *1CM to 2.5KM*

KEYMAP HEIGHTS SHOWN IN FEET

At-a-glance...

Walk	Page	Start	Distance	Time	Highest Point
Alloway and the Heads of Ayr	72	Alloway	10 miles (16.1km)	5 hrs	100ft (30m)
Ayr – Town, River and Valley	78	Ayr	10$\frac{1}{2}$ miles (16.9km)	5 hrs	197ft (60m)
Barr and the Water of Gregg	55	Changue Car Park	6$\frac{1}{2}$ miles (10.5km)	3$\frac{1}{2}$ hrs	853ft (60m)
Castle Semple Loch and Parkhill Wood	22	Castle Semple Loch	4 miles (6.4km)	2 hrs	197ft (60m)
Chatelherault and the Avon Gorge	33	Chatelherault Country Park	5 miles (8km)	2$\frac{1}{2}$ hrs	344ft (105m)
Clauchlands Point and Dun Fionn	63	Clauchlands	6 miles (9.7km)	3$\frac{1}{2}$ hrs	538ft (164m)
Coire-Fhionn Lochan	66	Thundergay	4 miles (6.4km)	2$\frac{1}{2}$ hrs	1082ft (330m)
Craignethan Castle and the Clyde Valley	68	Crossford	6$\frac{1}{2}$ miles (10.5km)	3$\frac{1}{2}$ hrs	485ft (148m)
Culzean Castle and Country Park	30	Culzean Country Park	3$\frac{1}{2}$ miles (5.6km)	2 hrs	164ft (50m)
Drumadoon Bay and King's cave	28	Blackwaterfoot	4$\frac{1}{2}$ miles (7.2km)	2$\frac{1}{2}$ hrs	148ft (45m)
Dunure	16	Dunure	1$\frac{1}{2}$ miles (2.4km)	1 hr	105ft (32m)
Goatfell	87	Brodick Castle Country Park or car park at Cladach	7 miles (11.3km)	6 hrs	2866ft (874m)
Great Cumbrae Island	26	Millport	4 miles (6.4km)	2 hrs	164ft (50m)
Greenock Cut and Shielhill Glen	75	Cornalees Bridge Visitor Centre	9 miles (14.5km)	4$\frac{1}{2}$ hrs	870ft (265m)
Kilchattan Bay, St Blane's Church	52	Kilchattan Bay	5$\frac{1}{2}$ miles (8.9km)	3$\frac{1}{2}$ hrs	515ft (157m)
Kildonan and Bennan Head	58	Kildonan	6$\frac{1}{2}$ miles (10.5km)	3 hrs	100ft (30m)
Kingarth and Dunagoil Fort	60	Kingarth	7$\frac{1}{2}$ miles (12.1km)	3$\frac{1}{2}$ hrs	164ft (50m)
Kyles of Bute	18	Ettrick Bay	3$\frac{1}{2}$ miles (5.6km)	1$\frac{1}{2}$ hrs	328ft (100m)
Largs	46	Largs	5$\frac{1}{2}$ miles (8.9km)	3 hrs	623ft (190m)
Machrie Moor Stone Circles	20	Area off A841 opposite Ashlar Farm or Historic Scotland sign	4 miles (6.4km)	2 hrs	128ft (39m)
Mugdock Country Park	40	Mugdock Country Park	5$\frac{1}{2}$ miles (8.9km)	2$\frac{1}{2}$ hrs	574ft (175m)
New Lanark and the Falls of Clyde	24	New Lanark	3$\frac{1}{2}$ miles (5.6km)	2 hrs	656ft (200m)
North Arran	84	South Newton	7$\frac{1}{2}$ miles (12.1km)	4$\frac{1}{2}$ hrs	862ft (263m)
Rothesay, Barone Hill and Loch Fad	43	Rothesay	5 miles (8km)	2$\frac{1}{2}$ hrs	531ft (162m)
Stinchar Falls	38	Stinchar Bridge Car Park	5$\frac{1}{2}$ miles (8.9km)	2$\frac{1}{2}$ hrs	1154ft (352m)
Straiton and Sclenteuch Moor	36	Straiton	4$\frac{1}{2}$ miles (7.2km)	2 hrs	705ft (215m)
Tinto Hill	82	Car park beyond Fallburn Farm off A73 SE of Lanark	4$\frac{1}{2}$ miles (7.2km)	2$\frac{1}{2}$ hrs	2334ft (711m)
Whiting Bay and Glenashdale Falls	49	Whiting Bay	6 miles (9.7km)	3 hrs	538ft (164m)

Comments

A short but absorbing 'Burns Trail' is followed by a walk along the Ayrshire coast to the impressive cliffs of the Heads of Ayr.

From the town centre of Ayr, you follow the river upstream to enjoy the pleasant and gently undulating countryside of the Ayr valley.

From many points on this walk on the edge of Carrick Forest, there are fine views across the Stinchar valley to the surrounding hills.

Attractive woodland is combined with a walk above and beside Castle Semple Loch in the Clyde Muirshiel Regional Park.

An attractive walk through a wooded gorge, once part of the hunting forest of the dukes of Hamilton, is combined with considerable historic interest.

From the highest point on the walk at Dun Fionn, the views over Brodick and Lamlash Bays, on the east coast of Arran, are superb.

A path beside a burn and waterfalls leads from Thundergay, on the north-west coast of Arran, to a beautiful and secluded loch cradled by hills.

Craignethan Castle occupies a fine position above the thickly-wooded Nethan Gorge, and there are extensive views over the Clyde Valley from several points on the walk.

There is much to explore and enjoy both in Culzean Castle and its surrounding park, and the views from the Cliff Walk near the end are outstanding.

A walk across fields and beside the shore on the west coast of Arran leads to an impressive cave associated with Robert the Bruce.

This short walk, on one of the wildest stretches of the Ayrshire coast, has a ruined castle as its focal point and grand views across to Arran.

This is the classic and popular walk up Goatfell. The views are magnificent but choose a fine day and take care on the scramble to the summit.

From this small island in the middle of the Firth of Clyde, the views across to the mainland and the other islands are magnificent.

There are extensive views across Greenock and the Firth of Clyde from the path beside the Greenock Cut. As a contrast, the last part of the walk is through a delightful wooded glen.

There is plenty of interest and variety on the walk at the south end of Bute. It includes a lovely stretch of coast, a secluded loch, a ruined church and a fine viewpoint.

From Kildonan, where the fine beach is overlooked by a ruined castle, you walk along the shore and below cliffs to the Black Cave at Bennan Head.

Sandy bays, woodland and two prehistoric monuments – standing stones and a vitrified fort – are the main ingredients of this walk at the south end of Bute.

A flat and easy walk that passes three historic sites and gives grand views across the Kyles of Bute to the Cowal peninsula.

The walk takes you up into the hills behind the coastal resort of Largs from where the views across to Bute, Arran and the Cumbraes are superb.

A fascinating and highly atmospheric walk near the west coast of Arran which embraces the most important group of prehistoric remains on the island.

Two ruined castles, woodland, grassland, an attractive loch and fine views make up an unusually interesting and varied walk.

The walk takes you from the fascinating and well preserved Industrial Revolution mill community along one side of the Clyde Gorge, passing a series of waterfalls.

After a short and relatively easy climb, followed by a descent to the coast, the remainder of the walk follows a beautiful and remote stretch of the North Arran coast back to Loch Ranza.

An easy climb to the summit of Barone Hill rewards you with grand views over Rothesay and the east coast of Bute.

A beautiful and well-waymarked trail through a remote part of Carrick Forest leads to a spectacular waterfall.

There are lovely views over the Girvan valley from the forested slopes of Sclenteuch Moor.

A straightforward climb leads to the summit of Tinto Hill and extensive views over the Clyde Valley and Southern Uplands.

Much of the walk is through forest and there are some grand views of the east coast of Arran, including Goatfell. The undoubted highlight is the spectacular Glenashdale Falls.

Introduction to Glasgow, the Clyde Valley, Ayrshire and Arran

Of all Britain's major provincial cities, Glasgow is the one that probably has the most immediate access to outstanding and unspoilt countryside. The Highlands start almost on the city's northern outskirts and the southern end of the West Highland Way, the end at which most walkers begin, is at Milngavie, one of Glasgow's residential suburbs. To the west and south-west of the city is Ayrshire, with its rolling hills, forested slopes, rugged coastline and sandy beaches. Beyond the Ayrshire coast lie the islands in the Firth of Clyde: Arran, Bute and the smaller islands of Great and Little Cumbrae.

Glasgow was originally a small cathedral city occupying a low ridge above the River Clyde, the seat of one of Scotland's two archbishoprics in the later Middle Ages. Its tremendous growth as a commercial and industrial city began in the early 18th century and in the 19th century it expanded even more rapidly, drawing into its booming shipyards thousands of workers from all parts of Scotland and immigrants from Ireland. At that time it was known as 'The Second City of the British Empire'. Its citizens – both the working classes crowded into often tightly packed and squalid tenements and the middle classes in their solid and spacious villas – sought escape, and the favourite excursions were to go 'doon the watter' by paddle-steamer or travel by train to the resorts on the Ayrshire coast or one of the Clyde islands. Now the traditional paddle-steamers have gone – except for one that is retained for tourist nostalgia – but visitors continue to come to these destinations by car, train and ferry.

This area, once the holiday playground for industrial Clydeside, has much to tempt walkers who might otherwise be more inclined to venture further north and west to the more obvious attractions of the Highlands or the Hebrides. Ayrshire is predominantly a region of rolling hills and expansive moorlands with wide river valleys and lush pastures. In the south many of the slopes are clothed with the conifer plantations of Carrick Forest, itself an extension of the Galloway Forest Park further south. There is plenty of fine walking in the hills, along the numerous forest trails and on the slopes of the Ayr, Doon, Girvan and Stinchar valleys.

Many would argue that the chief glory of Ayrshire is its rugged and often wild coastline, with impressive cliffs interspersed with fine sandy beaches. A series of ruined castles further enhances the scene and adds drama to the coastal landscape. The most visited castle, Culzean, is not however a sparse ruin but a grand 18th-century mansion designed by Robert Adam. It

Blackwaterfoot on the Isle of Arran

occupies a splendid clifftop position and both the castle and its grounds, now a country park, are owned by the National Trust for Scotland. Ayrshire is also renowned as 'Burns Country'. Scotland's national poet was born in a cottage at Alloway, just outside Ayr, in 1759 and the area is the setting for many of his works. The cottage and nearby sites associated with the poet's life have now become a Burns National Heritage Park.

Extending northwards from Ayrshire into Renfrewshire and the former shipbuilding towns along the south side of the Clyde is the Clyde Muirshiel Regional Park. This area of bare hills, windswept moorland, wooded glens and quiet lochs also provides plenty of varied routes for both walkers and cyclists, all within easy reach of Glasgow.

From many places, both on the Ayrshire coast and from the higher points of the Clyde Muirshiel Regional Park, the eye is drawn to the two principal islands lying offshore, Bute and Arran. There are some similarities between them. Both were popular with Glaswegians in the heyday of the Clyde paddle steamers, both have regular ferry services from the mainland and both are rich in prehistoric monuments. Also the Highland Boundary Fault, the break in the earth's crust that creates the geological boundary between Highland and Lowland Scotland, cuts across the islands which explains why, in both cases, the hillier and more rugged 'Highland' terrain is to be found in the north, and the gentler 'Lowland' scenery is in the south.

The more northerly of the two is Bute, its northern part almost enveloped by the 'fingers' of the Cowal peninsula from which it is separated by the narrow channels of the Kyles of Bute. Rothesay, the main town, is attractively situated on a sheltered bay and retains both a medieval castle and much of its impressive Victorian architectural heritage, a legacy of its heyday as a popular holiday resort.

There are no mountains on Bute. The bare moorlands in the north rise to no more than 900ft (274m) and the rest of the island is comparatively low lying with a pleasant pastoral landscape. The walking is pleasant and varied and there are especially fine coastal walks. From many points on the coast of Bute, the views across to the mainland, the Cowal and Kintyre peninsulas and the neighbouring islands are superb.

In contrast to Bute, Arran – or at least the northern half of the island – is mountainous, and none can fail to be impressed by the rugged profile of Goatfell and its neighbouring peaks as they approach Brodick Bay on the ferry. At 2866ft (874m) Goatfell is the highest peak in the Clyde area and both it and the adjacent peaks offer challenging and strenuous walking that requires a reasonable level of fitness and should not be underestimated.

Arran has often been described as Scotland in miniature and there is some justification in that accolade. The mountains in the north have a grandeur reminiscent of the best of Highland scenery, the coastline is magnificent and elsewhere there are wooded glens, forested hills, bare moorlands, remote lochs and dramatic waterfalls. The fact that all this is contained within an island that is no more than 20 miles (32.2km) long and 10 miles (16.1km) wide really does make Arran a walkers' paradise.

While it is easy to enthuse about the differing charms of the principal

Largs

islands, it should not be overlooked that there are other smaller islands in the firth. Great Cumbrae is easily and speedily reached by regular ferry service from Largs. Its one and only town, Millport, is situated on a sandy bay and possesses the smallest cathedral in Britain. As the island is fairly low, its walks reveal more outstanding and unimpeded views across the water to Bute, Arran and the mainland.

At first glance there would appear to be little to interest or excite the walker in the Clyde Valley to the south-east of Glasgow. This is one of the most heavily urbanised areas in Britain and was one of the chief centres of the Industrial Revolution, full of coalmines and steelworks. However, the mines and steelworks have gone, the whole area is much cleaner and greener and there are pleasant walks along the surprisingly unspoilt and tree-lined river. Dr Livingstone was born on the banks of the Clyde at Blantyre near Hamilton, and his birthplace, now the David Livingstone Centre, is well worth a visit.

South of Hamilton, industry is left behind and the river meanders through orchards and market gardens. There are more fine walks here, in the valleys of the Clyde and its tributary the Avon, and also on the nearby Tinto Hill, after Goatfell the next highest peak in this guide. Below Lanark the Clyde flows through a wooded gorge and over a series of falls upstream from the mill community of New Lanark. Such is the importance and historical significance of this well-preserved Industrial Revolution village, associated with the 19th-century social reformer Robert Owen, that it has been accorded the status of a World Heritage Site.

Squeezed between Dumfries and Galloway to the south and the Highlands and Hebrides to the north, and associated with coal-mining and heavy industry, the area around Glasgow tends to be overlooked by many walkers, apart from locals. As the following selection of walks reveal, it possesses a remarkable variety of both scenic and historic interest and has something to satisfy the needs of all walkers, from short and easy strolls to more strenuous and lengthier hikes. The only really challenging walks are the ascents of Goatfell and to a lesser extent Tinto Hill, but some of the other routes do have difficult stretches on uneven, rocky and muddy paths where care and patience is needed.

One final word about the weather: this part of Scotland has a relatively mild climate, protected by the long peninsula of Kintyre and influenced by the Gulf Stream. In some of the more sheltered parts of the east coasts of both Arran and Bute, first-time visitors may well be surprised to see palm trees growing, as along the promenades at Brodick and Rothesay. But there is also quite a high rainfall, and the weather can change suddenly, especially at the higher altitudes. Therefore even if you are only doing one of the short and easy walks, it is always advisable to have suitable footwear – ideally walking-boots – and take the appropriate clothing in case of rain or a sudden drop in temperature.

Dunure

Start	Dunure, Kennedy Park car park and picnic area
Distance	1½ miles (2.4km)
Approximate time	1 hour
Parking	Dunure
Refreshments	Pub and café at Dunure
Ordnance Survey maps	Landranger 70 (Ayr & Kilmarnock), Pathfinder 479, NS21/31 (Dunure & Dalrymple)

The village of Dunure is situated on a particularly wild stretch of the Ayrshire coast, and the ruins of its castle further enhance the drama of the scene. Although only a short walk, there are superb views along the coast in both directions and across the Firth of Clyde to the mountains of Arran and the Kintyre peninsula.

From the car park, walk along the top of the grassy, gorse-covered cliffs, in the direction of a green viewpoint waymark, and climb steps to the viewpoint. From here the magnificent view embraces Dunure Castle, a great sweep of the Ayrshire coast looking northwards to Ayr and southwards to Ailsa Craig, and across the Firth of Clyde to the Arran peaks and the long

Dunure Castle, Ayrshire

peninsula of Kintyre. A viewfinder enables you to identify the various places visible in clear conditions.

Just past the viewpoint, turn right down steps to the shingle beach and turn left along a path above it. The path bears slightly left into a meadow to continue above the shore and you follow it to the end of the meadow **A**. Ahead is another fine coastal view. Turn left and left again along the right edge of the meadow to pick up a track which heads gently uphill, passing along the upper edge of Kennedy Park, to emerge via a metal gate on to a road **B**.

Turn left downhill through the village and take the first turning on the left **C** to continue down to the attractive fishing harbour. At the end of a row of cottages turn left along a tarmac track and where the tarmac ends, turn left again between cottages. Follow the path to the right, passing to the right of limekilns, and continue over a burn and up steps to the 15th-century dovecote and beyond that to the castle ruins.

The gaunt ruins of Dunure Castle seem to match their wild and windswept surroundings perfectly. For centuries the castle was the seat of the Kennedys of Carrick, later earls of Cassillis, and in 1563 Gilbert Kennedy, the 4th earl, entertained Mary, Queen of Scots here. The same man was later responsible for probably the most bizarre event in the history of the castle, the roasting of Allan Stewart, Commendator of nearby Crossraguel Abbey, in an attempt to persuade him to hand over some of the abbey lands. Amazingly Stewart survived this ordeal and was rescued. From the castle the path leads back to the start. ●

SCALE 1:25000 or 2½ INCHES to 1 MILE 4CM to 1KM

| 0 | 200 | 400 | 600 | 800 METRES | 1 |
| 0 | 200 | 400 | 600 YARDS | ½ | KILOMETRES MILES |

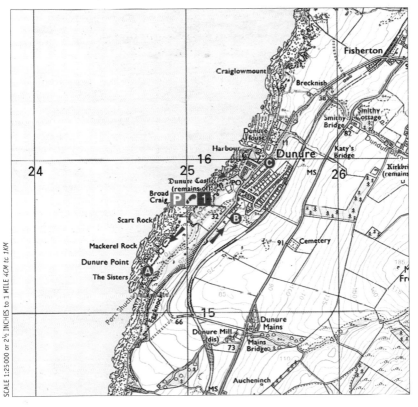

Along the shore of the Kyles of Bute

Start	Glecknabae Farm, at end of minor road to the north of Ettrick Bay
Distance	3½ miles (5.6km)
Approximate time	1½ hours
Parking	Parking area by entrance to Glecknabae Farm
Refreshments	None
Ordnance Survey maps	Landranger 63 (Firth of Clyde), Pathfinders 414, NS06/16 (Rothesay & Skelmorlie) and 400, NR87/97 (Tighnabruaich & Kilfinan)

From this flat and easy 'there and back' walk, along a delightful tree-lined track on the east coast of Bute, there are constantly outstanding views across the Kyles of Bute to the hills of Cowal and Arran. Along the way there are three historic sites to visit. The first two – St Michael's Grave and Glenvoidean Cairn – necessitate brief detours; the third, St Michael's Chapel, is at the half-way point.

Kyles of Bute

At the car park, go through a kissing-gate beside the track to Kilmichael and walk along this attractive, tree-lined track for nearly 1½ miles (2.4km) to Kilmichael Farm, passing through two gates. All the way there are the most superb views across the Kyles of Bute to the Cowal peninsula. The villages clearly visible on the other side of the water are Kames and Tighnabruaich.

After about 1 mile (1.6km), you make a brief detour to the left Ⓐ by walking across a field to a group of large stones occupying a low ridge. This is St Michael's Grave, a neolithic chambered cairn dating from around 4000 to 2000 BC. It gets its name from its proximity to St Michael's Chapel.

Return to the track which rises gently to pass a cottage and about 100 yds (91m) beyond it turn sharp right Ⓑ and

| U | 200 | 400 | 600 | 800 METRES | 1 | KILOMETRES |
| 0 | 200 | 400 | 600 YARDS | ½ | | MILES |

head up to a metal gate for the second, slightly lengthier detour. Go through the gate and continue uphill, following the track as it curves left, then right. At this point, keep ahead across the grass to Glenvoidean Cairn, identifiable by two prominent upright stones.

This is another neolithic chambered cairn, older and larger than the previous one. Its location on the side of the hill is superb, with magnificent views over the Kyles of Bute to Cowal, Kintyre and Arran. If you continue a little further up the track, the views become even better and you can enjoy impressive vistas ahead of the bare moorlands that cover much of this northern part of Bute.

Return to the track by the shore and continue to Kilmichael Farm. Just in front of the farm buildings, turn left through a metal gate, walk along the left edge of a field, by a wire fence on the left, turn left through another gate and head across the field to a circular enclosure **C**. Within this is a graveyard and the scanty remains of the medieval St Michael's Chapel. An iron gate admits you to the site. Although there is not much to see, the sparseness of the ruins is partly compensated for by the beautiful location above the Kyles of Bute almost opposite Kames.

From here retrace your steps along the tree-lined track to the starting point of the walk, enjoying more fine views, especially looking towards the Isle of Arran.

Machrie Moor Stone Circles

Start	Parking area on A841 almost opposite Ashlar Farm. There is a smaller parking area by the Historic Scotland sign to Machrie Moor Stone Circles about ½ mile (800m) to the north which reduces the walk by 1 mile (1.6km)
Distance	4 miles (6.4km) Shorter version 3 miles (4.8km)
Approximate time	2 hours (1½ hours for shorter walk)
Parking	Parking area opposite Ashlar Farm or small parking area by Historic Scotland sign for shorter walk
Refreshments	None
Ordnance Survey maps	Landranger 69 (Isle of Arran), Outdoor Leisure 37 (Isle of Arran)

Arran is rich in prehistoric remains and the greatest concentration of these is on Machrie Moor, on the west side of the island, which is littered with standing stones, burial chambers and stone circles. The walk enables you to see some of the most impressive of these remains, made more appealing and dramatic by their atmospheric setting on wild and open moorland partially enclosed by high hills. On the return leg there is the added bonus of fine views across Kilbrannan Sound to the long line of the Kintyre peninsula.

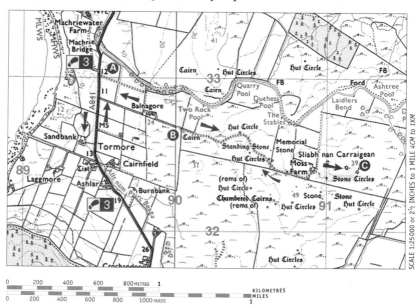

Machrie Moor Stone Circles

From the starting point at the parking area, turn right along the road as far as the Historic Scotland sign to the Machrie Moor Stone Circles and turn right over a stile **Ⓐ**. *The shorter walk starts at this point.*

Walk along a straight track, climb a stile and continue by the wire fence and trees on the left. The track bears right across the moorland and bends right, keeping alongside a wall on the left, to reach the field corner. Turn left over a stile **Ⓑ** and the Moss Farm Road Stone Circle is immediately ahead. This is a single row of granite boulders within which are the sparse remains of a Bronze Age burial cairn. It is uncertain if it was originally a stone circle with the later cairn built inside it, or a burial cairn provided with a stone enclosure.

Continue along the track which curves right and heads gently uphill to a low ridge. From here there are fine views all around of the encircling hills and more stones can be seen both to the left and right. Climb a stile, pass to the left of a stone circle and keep ahead – there is a ruined and abandoned farm to the left – to another stile. Climb that and continue to the prominent group of three standing stones, with more stone circles just beyond **Ⓒ**. The whole site is a complex one, with six circles in all, and has a marvellously atmospheric moorland setting between the hills and the sea.

From here retrace your steps across the moor to whichever of the two parking areas you started from. On this return leg there are grand views of the coast and across Kilbrannan Sound to Kintyre, and there are also imposing views to the right of Goatfell and its neighbouring peaks. ●

Castle Semple Loch and Parkhill Wood

Castle Semple Loch and Parkhill Wood

Start	Castle Semple Loch Visitor Centre, on the edge of Lochwinnoch
Distance	4 miles (6.4km) Shorter version 2½ miles (4km)
Approximate time	2 hours (1 hour for shorter walk)
Parking	Castle Semple Loch
Refreshments	Kiosk at the visitor centre
Ordnance Survey maps	Landranger 63 (Firth of Clyde), Pathfinders 429, NS 25/35 (Largs & Kilbirnie) and 415, NS 26/36 (Bridge of Weir)

A pleasant walk along the track of a disused railway is followed by a circuit of Parkhill Wood, beautiful at any time of the year but especially in spring when the ground is carpeted with bluebells. Then comes a detour along the track to see – at a distance only – the ruins of a 16th-century collegiate church. The final leg is along the shores of Castle Semple Loch. Views across the loch, both from the lochside path and from sections of the disused railway track, are superb. The short walk omits the detour to the church.

Begin by going up steps in front of the visitor centre and turn right along a tree-lined track. This is a disused railway track, part of the former Glasgow and South Western Railway, built in the early 1900s and now converted into a footpath and cycleway. After passing under a bridge, the track continues through a cutting and later come fine views to the right across Castle Semple Loch.

At a junction of paths and tracks **Ⓐ**, turn left through a gate to enter Parkhill Wood, a beautiful area of natural woodland. The path heads gently uphill beside the tumbling Blackditch Burn on the left and you keep along the main path all the while, later curving slightly right and continuing up to a metal gate **Ⓑ**. Do not go through it but turn left on to a path which winds gently downhill, crosses two small burns and continues through trees and bushes. The path then curves left over another burn, keeps ahead to cross another one and turns right to continue between burns on both sides. The main path can be seen over to the left and you cross the burn on the left and turn right to rejoin the outward route. Retrace your steps to the disused railway track **Ⓐ**.

The shorter walk crosses the track and continues through the gate opposite.

For the full walk, turn left along the track through another cutting and after about ¾ mile (1.2km) – where you

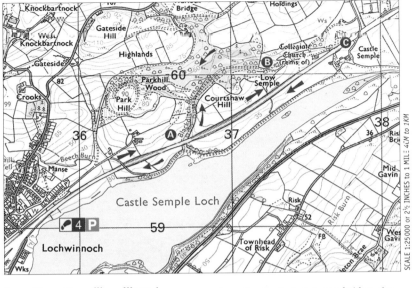

SCALE 1:25000 or 2½ INCHES to 1 MILE = 4CM to 1KM

```
0      200    400    600    800 METRES   1
                                          KILOMETRES
                                          MILES
0      200    400    600 YARDS   ½
```

emerge from the cutting for some more fine views across the loch – the ruined Castle Semple Collegiate Church can be seen in a field on the left. This was built in 1504 by John, 1st Lord Semple, who, like James IV and many of his countrymen, was killed at the Battle of Flodden in 1513. At present there is no access to the ruins. A little further on,

Parkhill Wood

where the track goes over a bridge, the few remains of Castle Semple, mostly the coach-house, can be seen on the right, incorporated within farm buildings **C**. The castle was built around 1500, demolished in the early 18th century and its site is now occupied by the farm.

Retrace your steps to the junction of paths and tracks by the entrance to Parkhill Wood **A**, turn left through a gate and continue down to the lochside. Turn right and follow a path beside the loch back to the visitor centre.   ●

New Lanark and the Falls of Clyde

Start	New Lanark
Distance	3½ miles (5.6km)
Approximate time	2 hours
Parking	New Lanark
Refreshments	Café at New Lanark Visitor Centre
Ordnance Survey maps	Landranger 71 (Lanark & Upper Nithsdale), Pathfinder 446, NS 84/94 (Lanark)

An extraordinary amount of both historic and scenic appeal is packed into this relatively short route. Historic interest is inevitably focused on the fascinating and well-preserved Industrial Revolution mill settlement of New Lanark, tucked away in the Clyde Valley. From here the walk proceeds upstream through the thickly-wooded Clyde Gorge, a Scottish Wildlife Trust Nature Reserve, passing a succession of falls. Make sure you leave plenty of time both to enjoy the walk through the gorge and to thoroughly explore New Lanark.

From the car park take the downhill tarmac path into New Lanark, turning sharp left near the bottom and descending steps to a road **A**. This successful and socially advanced industrial community was created by two remarkable men, David Dale and Robert Owen. It was founded in 1785 by Dale, a highly religious man and enlightened employer, but is particularly associated with Robert Owen who married Dale's daughter in 1799 and became the mill manager. Owen was in advance of his time; he had socialist leanings and believed in treating his workers decently and providing a better social environment for them.

Among his projects at New Lanark were the Nursery Buildings to house the pauper apprentices, the School for Children, based on the then unique philosophy of no punishments, and the Institute for the Formation of Character, a kind of early adult education college used for both educational and

New Lanark

recreational purposes. He also built good-standard housing and established the Village Store, run on co-operative principles with the profits being ploughed back into the village.

The three huge cotton mills – originally there were four – and rows of workers' cottages, all built from local sandstone and dating from the late 18th and early 19th centuries, are beautifully preserved and the unique interest of the site has deservedly given it World Heritage status. The former Institute is now a visitor centre where you can experience life in New Lanark around 1820, as told by a mill girl, and you can also see working cotton machines and visit the Village Store, restored mill workers' dwellings and Robert Owen's House.

Continue left along the road, turn right through gates into the mill complex, go down steps to the right of the visitor centre, cross a bridge over the Mill Lade and turn left along a tarmac drive. The drive bears right downhill, passing to the right of the Mechanics Workshop and under two arches. The first of the series of three falls – Dundaff Linn – is just ahead.

At a Clyde Walkway sign, turn left up a flight of steps, turn right under another arch and keep along the east side of the Clyde Gorge, following 'Falls of Clyde' signs all the time. The path ascends and descends steps and there are boardwalks in places as it continues through the thickly-wooded gorge. Bear right on joining a track **B** and at a fork in front of Bonnington Power Station, take the right-hand path. This hydroelectric power station was established in 1926 to harness the flow of the river.

Continue along the side of the gorge – there are more steps – and soon comes a fine view of the second falls, Corra Linn. Follow signs to Bonnington Linn

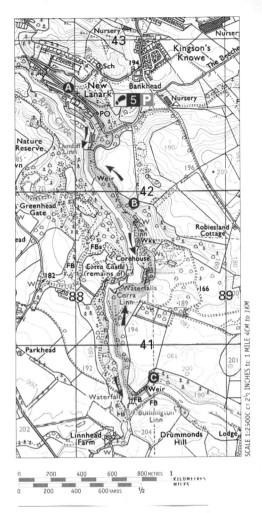

SCALE 1:25000 or 2½ INCHES to 1 MILE 4CM to 1KM

and now both sides of the gorge become almost perpendicular – on the other side of the river the meagre remains of Corra Castle can just be made out. The third fall, Bonnington Linn, comes into view and you continue as far as the bridge over the weir just beyond the fall, an excellent viewpoint **C**.

From here retrace your steps to where you first joined the track **B** – just beyond Bonnington Power Station – and continue along it, in the New Lanark direction. On reaching a T-junction just after crossing a burn, turn left and the track curves right into New Lanark. Walk through the village and retrace your steps up the tarmac path to the car park.

Great Cumbrae Island

Start	Millport
Distance	4 miles (6.4km)
Approximate time	2 hours
Parking	Millport – but a much cheaper alternative is to park at Largs, take the ferry across to Cumbrae Slip and use the shuttle bus service between the ferry terminal and Millport
Refreshments	Pubs and cafés at Millport
Ordnance Survey maps	Landranger 63 (Firth of Clyde), Pathfinder 428, NS05/15 (The Cumbraes)

Despite its name, Great Cumbrae is a small island in the Firth of Clyde, 'great' only in comparison with its much smaller neighbour of Little Cumbrae, and it has a distinct charm and atmosphere of its own. On the first part of the walk across fields to the west coast at Fintray Bay, the views over the water to the mainland and encircling islands and peninsulas are outstanding. The return is along the coast road, the B896, which is quieter than most country lanes and is highly scenic.

Millport is the only town on Great Cumbrae and, with its sheltered location at the south end of the island and sandy

Millport Harbour

bays, it was a popular destination when thousands of Glaswegians used to go 'doon the watter' by steamer to one of the Clyde resorts. Above the town and sheltered by trees is the tiny but

The Tan

SCALE 1:25000 or 2½ INCHES to 1 MILE 4CM to 1KM

0	200	400	600	800 METRES	1

KILOMETRES
MILES

0	200	400	600 YARDS	½

where the road ends, keep ahead along a tarmac track to Upper Kirkton Farm. In front of the farm buildings, turn left **A** along an enclosed track which bears right to a metal kissing-gate. Go through, turn first right and then left and walk alongside a wire fence on the right. After the fence ends, continue ahead across a field, keeping more or less in a straight line and going through a succession of gates. The views are genuinely magnificent: to the left is Bute, Arran and Kintyre, ahead is the Kyles of Bute, Cowal, Argyll and the southern edge of the Highlands, and to the right is the Ayrshire coast.

This splendid grassy path eventually descends to a gate. Go through, continue to descend between trees and bushes and go through a metal gate on to a road on the edge of Fintray Bay **B**. Turn left and follow this winding coast road, at the base of cliffs on the left, for 2½ miles (4km) back to Millport. Ahead the skyline is dominated by the imposing peaks of Arran and there are benches and picnic tables at intervals to enable you to enjoy the views in comfort.

On the edge of Millport – just after passing a small bay – turn right **C** along Millburn Street and turn left to a T-junction. Turn right again and follow the street as it bends left to return to the start.

●

charming Episcopal Cathedral of the Isles, the smallest cathedral in Britain and possibly in Europe. Designed in the Gothic style by the renowned Victorian architect William Butterfield, it was completed in 1851.

Begin at the pier and walk uphill along Cardiff Street. At a fork, turn right to continue gently uphill and

Drumadoon Bay and King's Cave

Start	Blackwaterfoot
Distance	4½ miles (7.2km)
Approximate time	2½ hours
Parking	Blackwaterfoot
Refreshments	Hotels at Blackwaterfoot, tearoom at Shiskine Golf and Tennis Club
Ordnance Survey maps	Landranger 69 (Isle of Arran), Outdoor Leisure 37 (Isle of Arran)

From Blackwaterfoot the route heads along the side of Drumadoon Bay, before crossing fields to reach the base of the prehistoric fort of The Doon or Drumadoon. It then continues beside the shore to King's Cave, both impressive in itself and a fine viewpoint. The cave has associations with Robert the Bruce. There are grand views looking across Kilbrannan Sound to the Kintyre peninsula.

Turn left out of the car park to cross the bridge over Black Water and where the road bends right **A**, keep ahead along a lane above Drumadoon Bay. Where the lane ends at the Shiskine Golf and Tennis Club, continue along a track – there is a public footpath sign to King's Cave – which keeps above the fine sandy beach.

The track bends right and then curves left across part of the golf course. At a sign to King's Cave, in front of redundant gateposts, turn left along the edge of the course, by a wire fence on the right, and look out for the next sign for King's Cave where you then turn right along a track **B** to a metal gate. Go through the gate, keep ahead across a field, go through a metal kissing-gate in the field corner and continue across the next field to a waymarked post at the base of the prominent hill of The

King's Cave

Doon, or Drumadoon, the site of an Iron Age fort **C**.

Bear left to descend below the end of the hill and turn right to follow a grassy path above the shore and below cliffs to King's Cave **D**. Approaching the caves, the path climbs slightly to pass across the face of the cliff. King's Cave, the furthest one along, with an iron railing across its entrance, is one of a number that are alleged to have provided shelter to Robert the Bruce. It is not thought to be the one in which, according to legend, he received inspiration from a spider. The cave overlooks a wild and dramatic stretch of coastline and there are impressive views across to Kintyre.

From here retrace your steps to the start.

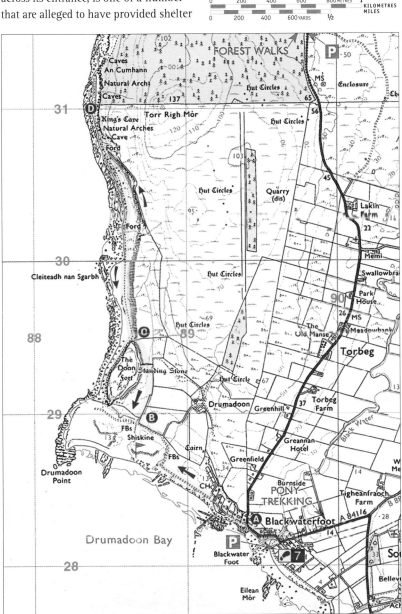

Culzean Castle and Country Park

Start	Culzean Country Park Visitor Centre
Distance	3½ miles (5.6km)
Approximate time	2 hours
Parking	Car park next to the visitor centre
Refreshments	Café at the visitor centre, kiosks throughout the park
Ordnance Survey maps	Landranger 70 (Ayr & Kilmarnock), Pathfinders 479, NS 21/31 (Dunure & Dalrymple) and 491, NS 20/30 (Maybole [South] & Dailly)

Although only a short walk, there is so much to see in the grounds of Culzean Castle, now a country park maintained by the National Trust for Scotland, that you could well devote most of the day to it. As well as the castle itself, there are many ancillary buildings plus such attractions as a Deer Park, Walled Garden and Swan Pond, all set amidst beautiful woodlands. Many would agree that the highlight of the route is the walk along the cliff path near the end. This winds through trees on the top of the cliffs, providing a series of magnificent views of the castle, along the wild and rugged Ayrshire coastline and across the Firth of Clyde to the mountains of Arran.

The walk begins in the circular courtyard of the visitor centre, imaginatively created from what was the Home Farm of the estate. Facing the sea, go through an archway on the left and walk along a path to a tarmac drive. Cross it and continue along the path, signposted 'Castle', which initially keeps parallel to the drive and emerges on to another drive by the Ruined Arch and Viaduct. This was designed by Robert Adam to form a romantic and imposing entrance to Culzean Castle. The castle is just to the right but is best left to near the end of the walk.

Walk along the drive – or along the parallel path to the right of it – to the Walled Garden. To the left is the Deer Park, originally much larger than at present, and a brief detour to the right brings you to the Camellia House, designed as an orangery in 1818. In front of the Walled Garden – well worth an exploration – take the tarmac drive which turns left **A** and heads gently uphill through woodland, keeping on the main drive all the while. On reaching a long, low white building, formerly a mill, the drive turns first left and then right around the end of the building. Keep ahead along a rough track gently downhill into woodland, bending right and continuing under a disused railway bridge.

Immediately turn right on to a path to join the tree-lined track of the

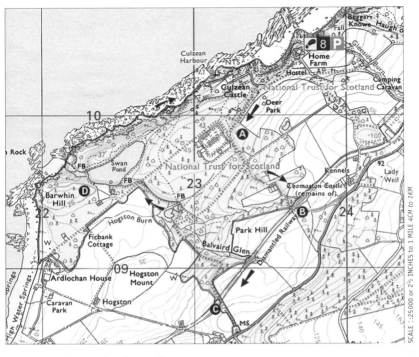

SCALE ::25000 or 2½ INCHES to 1 MILE 4CM to 1KM

```
0      200    400    600    800 METRES   1
                                          KILOMETRES
                                          MILES
0      200    400    600 YARDS           ¼
```

disused railway **B**, operational between 1906 and 1955, and keep along it as far as a bridge. To the right are grand views across the Firth of Clyde to Arran. Climb the steps to the right of the bridge, turn right **C** along a track and head gently downhill, under an impressive beech-lined canopy, to pass through the Cat Gates, one of the entrances to the estate and guarded by stone cats.

Pass through the gates and at a fork about 50 yds (46m) ahead, take the left-hand path to reach a crossroads. Turn left, beside a burn on the right, cross a drive and continue along the path to the Swan Pond, a most attractive and popular part of the park. Turn left alongside the pond, continue across grass to pick up a path again and at a sign to Port Carrick and Barwhin Hill turn left for a brief detour, descending steps to the fine beach at Port Carrick.

Return to the path beside the pond, turn left along it, cross a footbridge and continue along the uphill path ahead. Take the first path on the left **D** – this is the Cliff Walk – and follow a winding, undulating path through woodlands on top of the cliffs. This is a most memorable part of the walk, with magnificent views along the Ayrshire coast and across the sea to the mountains of Arran and the long line of the Kintyre peninsula beyond. At a T-junction, turn left to continue above the sea and now come impressive views of Culzean Castle ahead. Take the left-hand path at a fork and continue across grass towards the castle. Turn right through a gate, go down steps and turn left to walk across the Fountain Court in front of the castle.

Splendidly situated on a precipitous cliff above the Firth of Clyde, Culzean Castle was originally a tower-house belonging to the Kennedys of Carrick, later the earls of Cassillis, of nearby Dunure. After Dunure Castle fell into ruin, it became their principal residence and, in keeping with its new status, it was completely reconstructed for the 10th earl by the renowned Scottish architect Robert Adam between 1777 and 1792. It is basically an elegant Georgian country house but Adam included some medieval-looking towers and turrets to give it a more castle-like appearance. In 1946 General Eisenhower was given a flat on the top floor in gratitude for his role in the Allied victory in World War II; this flat is now an Eisenhower museum.

At the far end of the Fountain Court, turn right across grass and pass under the arch of the viaduct seen earlier. Keep walking ahead to join a tarmac drive and follow it back to the visitor centre.

Culzean Castle

Chatelherault and the Avon Gorge

Start	Chatelherault Country Park, off A72 near Ferniegair to the south of Hamilton
Distance	5 miles (8km) Shorter version 3½ miles (5.6km)
Approximate time	2½ hours (1½ hours for shorter walk)
Parking	Chatelherault Country Park
Refreshments	Café at the visitor centre
Ordnance Survey maps	Landranger 64 (Glasgow, Motherwell & Airdrie), Pathfinder 431, NS65/75 (Hamilton)

Almost the whole of this highly attractive walk is either along the edge of, or through the beautiful woodlands that clothe the sides of the Avon Gorge, sometimes above and sometimes below the river. The country park is based on Chatelherault, a former hunting-lodge of the dukes of Hamilton, and there is plenty of historic interest in the restored lodge itself, the nearby scanty ruins of Cadzow Castle and the Duke's Monument. All the paths are clear, well surfaced and well signposted. The shorter version of the walk omits the detour to the Duke's Monument.

There is nothing Scottish sounding about Chatelherault. The name is that of a French duchy, a gift from the French king to the Hamilton family for helping to arrange the betrothal of Mary, Queen of Scots to the dauphin in 1548. The house was built in the 18th century as a hunting lodge and summerhouse for the 5th duke of Hamilton and was part of an overall design, linked to Hamilton Palace by a Grand Avenue of trees. Mining subsidence led to the demolition of Hamilton Palace in the 1920s, and Chatelherault fell into ruin after World War II. It was restored as a museum in the 1980s, and part of the High Parks estate, formerly a royal and later a ducal hunting forest, became a country park. Although the palace has gone, the view from the front of the lodge is still impressive, stretching northwards across the park to Hamilton and the 18th-century mausoleum, and beyond that to the urbanised Clyde Valley on the fringes of Glasgow.

The walk begins in front of the visitor centre, which was once the kennels for the hunting dogs. Facing the building, turn left along a tarmac path, signposted 'Riverside Walks'. The path heads gently downhill, does a U-bend to the left, continues down and bends right to cross the Duke's Bridge high above the River Avon. From here there are fine views both up and down the river. Head uphill and bend right to pass to the left of the scanty remains of Cadzow Castle, believed to have been

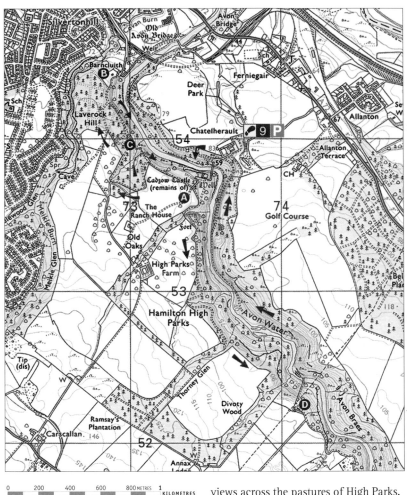

built in the early 16th century by James Hamilton, who also built the nearby Craignethan Castle.

After passing the castle, follow the tarmac path around a left bend to a T-junction of paths in front of a gate **Ⓐ**.

For the short walk, turn left here in the 'Cadzow Oaks and White Bridge' direction.

The full version of the walk makes a detour to the Duke's Monument. Turn right at the T-junction on to a path which twists and turns, keeping along the top-left inside edge of woodland for most of the time. To the left are fine

views across the pastures of High Parks, dotted with some of the ancient Cadzow Oaks. On reaching a sign to the Duke's Monument, bear right along a tarmac drive to the Grecian-style memorial, **Ⓑ** erected in honour of the 11th duke of Hamilton. After his death in 1863, £1500 was raised by friends and tenants and the dramatic site above the Avon Gorge was chosen by his wife because it commanded a view of both Chatelherault and the former ducal palace. The bronze bust of the duke was moved to the courtyard of the visitor centre for safety.

Walk back along the drive and at the first sign to Chatelherault and Cadzow Castle – where the drive curves right –

keep ahead along a path through woodland to a T-junction **C**. Turn left – here picking up the earlier route – and retrace your steps to the T-junction where you rejoin the shorter walk **A**.

Keep ahead along an enclosed path to a T-junction and turn right to join the Avon Walkway. Follow an attractive and well-surfaced path which twists and turns along the top-right edge of woodland above the Avon Gorge for nearly 1 ½ miles (2.4km). The path passes through mixed broad-leaved and conifer woodland and there are more fine views to the right of some of the ancient Cadzow Oaks.

Chatelherault

At a sign 'White Bridge and Chatelherault', turn left **D** on to a path into the trees and at a fork, continue along the left-hand path which descends, via steps and more twists and turns, to cross the White Bridge over the River Avon. This is another delightful spot, with more grand views both up- and downstream. On the other side the path turns left to keep alongside or just above the river through more beautiful mixed woodland.

Later the path ascends to a fork by a stand of Douglas Fir. At this point continue along the right-hand upper path, heading gently uphill through dark conifers to a gate. Pass beside it and turn right to return to the start. ●

Straiton and Sclenteuch Moor

Straiton and Sclenteuch Moor

Straiton and Sclenteuch Moor

Start	Straiton
Distance	4½ miles (7.2km)
Approximate time	2 hours
Parking	Straiton
Refreshments	Pub and café at Straiton
Ordnance Survey maps	Landranger 77 (Dalmellington to New Galloway), Pathfinder 491, NS 20/30 (Maybole [South] & Dailly)

This is a straightforward 'up, across, down and across' walk amidst the attractive scenery of the Girvan valley. From Straiton, the route heads up to the forested slopes of Sclenteuch Moor to the north of the village, continues through a conifer plantation and descends to a lane for the final stretch back to the start. The views over the valley and surrounding hills are outstanding.

With a street of old stone cottages and an 18th-century church, Straiton is a most appealing village. Its attractive location, beside the Water of Girvan and cradled by hills, makes it a fine walking centre.

For the whole of the walk you follow yellow waymarks. Start by turning left out of the car park and almost immediately turn right along a tarmac

Girvan valley, near Straiton

drive called Fowlers Croft. The drive becomes first a rough track and, after passing the last of a group of cottages, an enclosed path that keeps alongside a burn on the right. Turn right to cross a footbridge over the burn and then turn left along a lane. After about 200 yds (183m), turn left **Ⓐ** to recross the burn and walk along a steadily ascending tarmac track, once part of an old drove road. After passing a cottage on the left, it continues as a rough track up to the edge of Sclenteuch Moor Plantation.

At the edge of the wood, turn left over a ladder stile **Ⓑ** and follow a path through the conifers to a T-junction. Gaps in the trees reveal fine views over to the left across the Girvan valley. Turn left at the T-junction along a track which bends to the left and continues winding through the conifers. A way-marked forest trail will take you on through the trees to a burn which can be crossed by a small, almost hidden, footbridge, before rejoining the path. Eventually the path emerges from the woodland, bends sharply left and keeps along the right edge of the trees. Descend gently, re-entering the plantation, and continue down to a gate. Go through, descend more steeply and turn right in front of a farmyard.

Pass to the right of a bungalow and then turn left to continue downhill along a tarmac track to a road. **Ⓒ** Turn left and follow the road back to the village of Straiton.

0	200	400	600	800 METRES	1
					KILOMETRES
					MILES
0	200	400	600 YARDS	½	

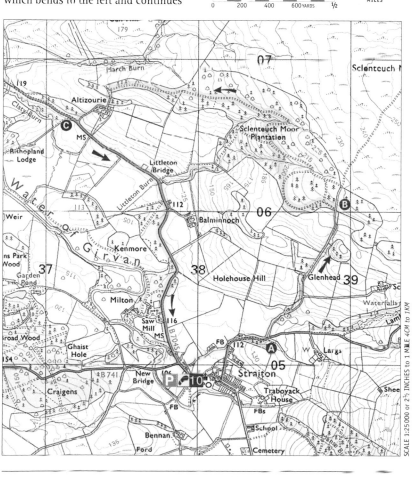

SCALE 1:25000 or 2½ INCHES to 1 MILE 4CM to 1KM

Stinchar Falls

Start	Forestry Commission's Stinchar Bridge car park, on minor road between Straiton and Bargrennan
Distance	5½ miles (8.9km)
Approximate time	2½ hours
Parking	Stinchar Bridge car park
Refreshments	None
Ordnance Survey maps	Landranger 77 (Dalmellington to New Galloway), Outdoor Leisure 32 (Galloway Forest Park)

Much of this delightful walk through part of Carrick Forest keeps beside the River Stinchar, passing a succession of small cascades. About half-way round are the larger and more impressive Stinchar Falls, seen from a viewing platform above them. The route is well waymarked and easy to follow but, despite the provision of boardwalks in places, expect some of the paths to be soft and muddy.

In Carrick Forest

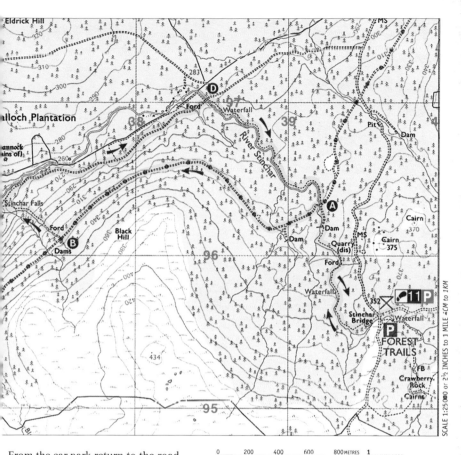

SCALE 1:25 000 or 2½ INCHES to 1 MILE 4CM to 1KM

From the car park return to the road, cross over and take the path opposite, signposted 'Stinchar Falls'. There are frequent signs and you follow blue-ringed posts throughout. The path keeps along the right bank of the River Stinchar, follows it round a right bend, crosses a footbridge over a burn and continues – there are boardwalks in places – to reach a broad track just to the right of a bridge **A**.

Turn left over the bridge and keep along the track for nearly 1½ miles (2.4km). Where the conifers have been cleared, there are fine views ahead and to the right across the forest to the surrounding hills. At a sign 'Falls', turn right **B** on to a path that descends quite steeply through tightly packed conifers, by a burn on the left, to the viewing-platform above the Stinchar

Falls **C**. When in full spate after heavy rain, they make an impressive sight as the water surges over the rocks below.

From the platform turn right and head up to a sign 'Walk Continues'. The path keeps above the river and later widens into a clear and steadily ascending track. After crossing a bridge over the river, turn right **D**, at a sign 'Stinchar Walk This Way', on to a path that keeps beside the river, across more boardwalks, following it around two right bends to a track. This is a delightful part of the walk with plenty of places to stop for a picnic.

Cross the track and keep ahead **A**, here rejoining the outward route, to retrace your steps to the start. ●

Mugdock Country Park

Start	Mugdock Country Park, Craigend Visitor Centre, signposted from the A81 just to the north of Milngavie
Distance	5½ miles (8.9km)
Approximate time	2½ hours
Parking	Craigend Visitor Centre
Refreshments	Café at Craigend Visitor Centre
Ordnance Survey maps	Landranger 64 (Glasgow, Motherwell & Airdrie), Pathfinder 403, NS 47/57 (Clydebank & Milngavie) Outdoor Leisure 39 (Loch Lomond)

Considerable variety is packed into this relatively short but thoroughly absorbing walk. It takes in some beautiful woodlands, areas of open grassland, a loch and a reservoir, two ruined castles – one medieval and the other 19th century – and a stretch of the West Highland Way. From many points on the route there are views of the Campsie Fells and Kilpatrick Hills, and occasional glimpses of tower blocks – a reminder that Glasgow is surprisingly close.

The walk starts in front of the visitor centre, built in the early 19th century as the stable block for Craigend Castle. Do not take the path signposted 'Mugdock Castle and Loch, Craigend Castle' but the one to the left of it that heads into trees and passes along the right edge of a small loch. Keep ahead at a cross-roads, descending gently and going over two plank footbridges, and the path continues along the right edge of Pheasant's Wood, by a wire fence on the right.

At a sign to Mugdock Castle, turn right (still with a wire fence on the right) across the open grassland of Peitches Moor, making for the belt of trees ahead, and cross a footbridge to reach a crossroads. Turn left along a tree-lined track and take the first turning on the right **Ⓐ** to continue along a path across marshy ground –

fortunately it is mostly on boardwalks – towards the mound of Mugdock Castle. Turn right at a T-junction in front of the mound, follow the base of it as it curves left to another T-junction and turn left along a track to pass in front of the castle. Mugdock Castle, which occupies a commanding position above the loch, was the principal seat of the powerful Graham family, later the earls of Montrose, who, over several centuries, played a prominent role in Scottish politics, and in the many conflicts between England and Scotland. Most of the existing ruins are of the original 14th-century fortress, with some later additions.

The track curves left, gently descends to the shores of Mugdock Loch and continues through trees, by a burn on the left. Turn left to cross the burn, go through a gate to leave the park and

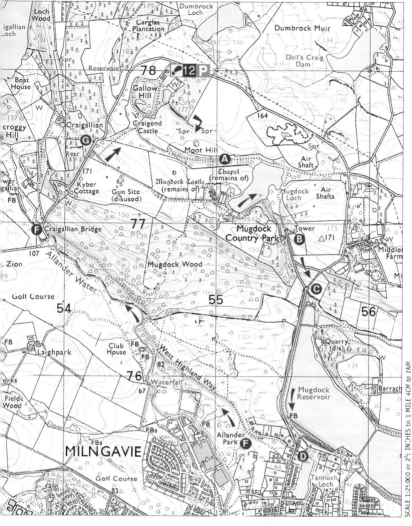

0	200	400	600	800 METRES	1

KILOMETRES
MILES

0	200	400	600 YARDS	½

turn right along a broad track. **B** The track becomes first a lane and then a road which heads downhill to Mugdock Reservoir. You can continue along the road but it is more pleasant – if marginally longer – to turn left **C** through a metal gate and turn right along a path that runs between the road and the reservoir. The path follows the curve of the reservoir to the left and keeps above it to emerge on to a water authority road. To the right are views over the built up area of Milngavie and the small Tannoch Loch.

Turn sharp right along the road which descends below the reservoir, curves left and goes through a metal gate to rejoin the previous road on the edge of Milngavie. Keep ahead along it for a few yards and turn right **D** along Drumclog Avenue. Where the road bears right, bear left along a short section of path to a T-junction, turn right and at the next junction of paths a few yards in front, keep ahead, in the direction of Mugdock Wood, to join the West Highland Way **E**.

Mugdock Wood

Follow a well-constructed, winding, tree-lined and attractive path into Mugdock Wood and continue through this beautiful area of woodland, above Allander Water on the left, to eventually emerge, via a kissing-gate, on to a lane **F**. Turn right steeply uphill, following the lane through mixed woodland around two sharp bends, and at the top comes a grand view ahead of the Campsie Fells.

Just where the lane starts to descend, turn right **G** along a track to re-enter the country park – there is a sign here to Kyber Car Park – and turn left through a kissing-gate on to a path signposted 'Visitor Centre and Craigend Castle'. Follow this path to a T-junction by Craigend Castle. These rather forlorn-looking remains are of a Gothic Revival house, built for the Smith family, the lairds of Craigend, in the early 19th century. Between 1949 and 1956 there was a zoo within the grounds.

At the T-junction, turn left along a track which winds through woodland back to the start. ●

Rothesay, Barone Hill and Loch Fad

Start	Rothesay, Isle of Bute
Distance	5 miles (8km)
Approximate time	2½ hours
Parking	Rothesay
Refreshments	Pubs and cafés at Rothesay
Ordnance Survey maps	Landranger 63 (Firth of Clyde), Pathfinder 414, NS06/16 (Rothesay & Skelmorlie)

From the centre of Rothesay the walk heads up over Barone Hill, the prominent landmark to the south-west of the town, 531ft (162m) high and a superb viewpoint. After descending, the route continues through woodland adjoining Loch Fad and crosses a causeway over the loch, another fine viewpoint. From here a farm track and roads lead back to the start. Short sections of the walk are across rather boggy and badly drained ground

In Victorian times and as late as the 1950s, the Clyde steamers used to bring thousands of holidaymakers to Rothesay from the city of Glasgow and the neighbouring towns. The town still has a pleasantly old-fashioned atmosphere with large, solid and dignified Victorian villas lining the bay (originally built by wealthy Glaswegian merchants) a fine glass and steel Winter Gardens and the most ornate public conveniences in the country; the latter were recently restored and are now regarded as a historic monument.

Rothesay's history goes back much further. The castle, a favourite residence of the Stuart kings, was built in the 13th century. It has an unusual circular shape and mainly comprises a curtain wall surrounded by a moat. The fore-work, a tower jutting out into the moat, was added by James IV and James V in the 16th century. During its turbulent

history it has suffered many sieges – the earliest recorded one by Norwegians in 1230. It was finally destroyed in the 17th century by a combination of English and Highland troops, but was restored in the 19th century.

Start at the pier and with your back to the harbour, walk up High Street, passing to the left of the castle. Follow the castle moat to the right to continue along Stuart Street and at a T-junction, turn left. Turn right at a crossroads and after ¼ mile (400m) – just after the road curves right and starts to climb – turn left **Ⓐ** on to a road which bears right to continue along the right edge of a recreation ground.

Keep ahead along a tarmac drive, pass beside a barrier and immediately turn right along a path beside tennis-courts on the left. Follow this path across the park, go up steps to a T-junction and turn right along an

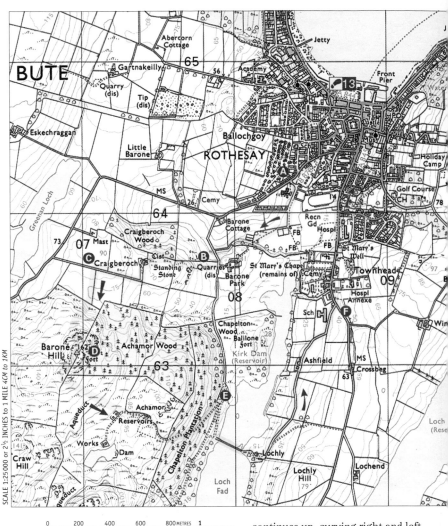

attractive, tree-lined path beside a cut on the left. This channel, called the Lovers' Walk Cut, was constructed by Robert Thom, the civil engineer famed for the much longer Greenock Cut above the Clyde.

The path emerges on to a lane. Turn left, and at a footpath sign to Barone Hill turn right **B** through a gate and head gently uphill across a field, making for a wall on the left. The path – not always obvious – curves right between gorse and trees, bends left and continues up, curving right and left again and heading across rough grass to a kissing-gate in the top left-hand corner. Go through and continue in the same direction through more gorse bushes, bearing left away from a wall bordering woodland on the right, to a standing stone.

Head towards Craigberoch Farm, keeping to the left of the derelict farm buildings, and turn left on to a track. The track bends right, climbs gently, then levels off and, just before it starts to descend, turns left through a gate, **C**. Walk along the left edge of rough pasture by a wire fence on the left,

Rothesay Castle

climb a ladder-stile and cross a plank footbridge. Now comes a steep climb up between rocky outcrops to the triangulation pillar on the summit of Barone Hill. **D** From here the views are magnificent, extending across Bute to Arran and Cowal.

Keep ahead past the triangulation pillar to descend by a wall on the left and after about 200 yds (183m) turn left over a ladder-stile and head downhill towards the left edge of water treatment buildings where you join a tarmac track. Bear left and follow it as it winds downhill, initially across open moorland and later through conifer woodland, to a T-junction **E**.

Turn right and at a fork immediately in front take the left-hand track, signposted 'Birdhide and Loch Fad', which continues through attractive woodland bordering the loch.

Turn left to cross a causeway over Loch Fad, enjoying the fine views on both sides, and continue along a gently ascending track. The track bends left and continues, past farms and finally a school, to a road **F**. Turn left and follow the road back to the start. On the left you pass St Mary's Chapel, the only surviving part of Rothesay's medieval parish church, next to the High Kirk. In the church grounds is the Bute family mausoleum. The road continues along the right edge of a recreation ground and on past the castle to the pier. ●

Largs

Start	Largs
Distance	5½ miles (8.9km) Shorter version 4 miles (6.4km)
Approximate time	3 hours (2 hours for shorter walk)
Parking	Largs
Refreshments	Pubs and cafés at Largs
Ordnance Survey maps	Landranger 63 (Firth of Clyde), Pathfinder 429, NS25/35 (Largs & Kilbirnie)

The route takes you up into the hills above Largs, from where the views across the Firth of Clyde to the Cumbraes, Bute, Arran and Cowal are magnificent. After returning to the edge of the town, the walk heads down into the wooded Gogo Glen and this is followed by a short stretch of suburban walking to reach Douglas Park, where there is a prehistoric tomb. Finally comes a relaxing stroll by the sea along a traffic-free promenade. The shorter route returns directly to the start and omits Gogo Glen, Douglas Park and the promenade walk.

Dignified Victorian terraces set well back from the shore, imposing red sandstone 19th-century churches, lawns leading down to the promenade and a good selection of pubs, restaurants and tearooms, are a reflection of the heyday of Largs as a fashionable Clydeside resort. It is still a popular destination, and Vikingar, the town's latest attraction, makes use of the latest technology to bring to life the history of the Vikings in Scotland. Off the main street is the elaborate 17th-century Skelmorlie Aisle, built as a mausoleum, the only surviving part of the Auld Kirk.

Start by the Great Cumbrae ferry terminal and, with your back to the pier, keep ahead along the main street. At a fork take the left-hand road (Tron Place), turn left at a T-junction and at the next T-junction turn right into

Gateside Road. Keep ahead at a crossroads along Flatt Road, climbing steadily and passing to the right of school buildings, and at a T-junction, turn right along Bellesdale Avenue. The road bears left and, just before reaching the last of the houses, bear left **Ⓐ** on to an uphill tarmac track to a metal gate.

Go through, continue steeply uphill, going round a left and then a right bend, and where the track bends left again, keep ahead along a path to a stile. Climb it, continue ascending steadily above Gogo Glen on the right, climb another stile and keep ahead, with fine views in front of bare, grassy slopes. The path later curves left, descends and then turns right to Greeto Bridge **Ⓑ**, a beautiful spot where the tributary burn of Greeto Water tumbles down a series of cascades to meet Gogo Water.

SCALE 1:25000 or 2½ INCHES to 1 MILE 4CM to 1KM

```
0      200    400    600    800 METRES  1
                                        KILOMETRES
                                        MILES
0      200    400    600 YARDS   ½
```

From here retrace your steps to where you left the road **A** on the edge of Largs. As you descend, the views ahead over the town and across the Firth of Clyde to Great Cumbrae, Bute and the peaks of Arran are awe-inspiring.

On reaching the road, return to the start if doing the shorter walk.

For the full walk, turn sharp left and, where the road ends, keep ahead for a few yards along a track to a fork and take the right-hand track which heads gently downhill through the woodland of Gogo Glen. At the bottom turn sharp right **C** on to a path beside the burn and, after emerging from the trees, keep ahead, passing to the left of a large house. Turn left to cross a bridge over the burn and go through a metal gate.

Now follows a short stretch of suburban road walking. Turn right, take the first turning on the left and where the road ends, go up steps to join another road. Turn right, after a few yards turn left into Castlehill Drive, turn right at a T junction and take the second road on the left (Cunningham Drive). Turn right at a T-junction and at the next one, turn left along the main road **D**.

After a few yards, turn left through a metal gate into Douglas Park. Walk along the left edge of a bowling-green, go under an arch and up steps to continue through the colourful Burns Garden and follow the path round to the right and through a gate. Turn left on to a tarmac drive which bends right, in the Haylie Chambered Tomb direction and, where the drive peters out, continue across grass, by an iron fence on the left and beside a metal gate, to reach the tomb **E**. This prehistoric burial chamber is alleged to date from around 3000 BC.

Retrace your steps through the park and continue down the tree-lined, tarmac drive to go through the main gates on to the road. Cross over and, almost opposite, go through the gates of the Anderson Memorial Park. Walk along a tarmac path, keeping to the right of a childrens' play-area, and at a T-junction turn left and go through a metal gate on to a road (May Street).

Turn right and, with a fine view ahead over Great Cumbrae, walk down to the promenade.

To the left the Pencil Monument can be seen. This was erected in 1912 to commemorate victory over the Vikings at the Battle of Largs in 1263, a victory which marked the end of Viking control over the west of Scotland. Turn right **F** along the tarmac promenade and follow it back to the start, for a pleasant and relaxing finale to the walk. ●

Greeto Water, above Largs

Whiting Bay and Glenashdale Falls

Start	Whiting Bay, car park at north end of bay near the church
Distance	6 miles (9.7km)
Approximate time	3 hours
Parking	North end of Whiting Bay
Refreshments	Hotels and cafés at Whiting Bay
Ordnance Survey maps	Landranger 69 (Isle of Arran), Outdoor Leisure 37 (Isle of Arran)

From the north end of Whiting Bay on the east coast of Arran, attractive forest paths and tracks bring you to the spectacular Glenashdale Falls. The route continues along the side of the wooded valley, gradually descending to follow Glenashdale Burn to its mouth at the south end of the bay. A mixture of lanes, paths and wooded tracks lead back to the start, passing by the Fairy Glen. This is a relatively easy walk along well-defined paths and tracks, with no strenuous sections and some fine views of Holy Island and along the coast.

From the car park walk back to the main road, turn left and take the first turning on the right, signposted 'Cart Track, Knockenkelly and Auchencairn'. The tarmac track heads uphill, becoming first a rough hedge and tree lined track and then narrowing to a path, to join a track.

As you bear right along this track, there are grand views to the right along the coast, with the prominent landmark of Goatfell in the background. Just after passing farm buildings, turn sharp left **Ⓐ**, at a sign 'Forest Path', on to a path which winds uphill through conifers – dark and gloomy in places – to reach a T-junction **Ⓑ**. A detour of about 50 yds (45m) to the right here brings you to a superb viewpoint overlooking the bay, Holy Island, the Goatfell range and

across the Firth of Clyde to the mainland.

The route continues to the left to follow an undulating track through the forest for about 1½ miles (2.4km). At a sign to Whiting Bay and Glenashdale Falls, turn left **Ⓒ** along a track and just after a left bend, turn right, at a Glenashdale Falls sign, on to a path which heads down through more dark conifers to a T-junction. Turn right and the path immediately bends left and continues through the trees to cross a footbridge over Glenashdale Burn at the top of the falls **Ⓓ**.

After crossing the bridge, turn left to keep high above the burn, turn left after crossing another bridge and descend steps. Turn right at a 'Viewpoint' sign, continue downhill and at the next

SCALE 1:25 000 or 2½ INCHES to 1 MILE 4CM to 1KM

'Viewpoint' sign, turn left for a brief detour down to the most impressive view of the falls. Here the burn plunges over 120ft (36m) in a spectacular double cascade into the narrow wooded gorge.

Return to the path which continues along the side of the gorge, later descending to keep beside the burn. Pass beside a fence and keep ahead along a track to emerge on to a road at the south end of Whiting Bay **E**. Turn left over Ashdale Bridge, walk beside the shore and at a public footpath sign to Glenashdale Falls turn left along a lane **F**. The lane ascends, bends right, then turns left and continues uphill to a crossroads. Turn right **G**, in the Fairy Glen, Knockenkelly and Auchencairn direction and, shortly after passing the clubhouse of the Whiting Bay Golf Club, where the lane peters out, continue along a track signposted to

Fairy Glen. Go through a metal gate, turn right to cross a footbridge over a burn – this is the Fairy Glen – and continue between bushes, descending to cross another burn. Keep ahead and go through a metal gate on to a track **Ⓗ**.

Turn left and at the fork immediately in front, take the left-hand track which heads uphill and curves right. Keep along this attractive tree-lined track for ½ mile (800m), and about 100 yds (91m) after passing a Knockenkelly Farm and a row of cottages look out for where you turn sharp right on to a downhill path.

At this point you rejoin the outward route and retrace your steps to the starting point. ●

Overlooking Lamlash Bay

Kilchattan Bay, St Blane's Church and Suidhe Chatain

Start	Kilchattan Bay
Distance	5½ miles(8.9km)
Approximate time	3½ hours
Parking	By the pier at Kilchattan Bay
Refreshments	Hotel at Kilchattan Bay
Ordnance Survey maps	Landranger 63 (Firth of Clyde), Pathfinder 428, NS05/15 (The Cumbraes)

This superbly beautiful and varied walk takes you around the south end of Bute. Soon after reaching Glencallum Bay, it turns inland, passes the mysterious-looking Loch na Leighe and continues to the highly atmospheric remains of St Blane's Church. The final leg is over Suidhe Chatain, which reaches a height of 515ft (157m), affording memorable views which encompass a large part of Bute, plus the coasts of Ayrshire and Cowal and the islands of Arran and the Cumbraes. The coast path on the first part of the walk is rocky in places but should present no problems and there may be muddy paths elsewhere. Pick a fine day and take your time as this is a walk to be savoured to the full.

The walk begins at the pier at Kilchattan Bay. Facing the sea, turn right along the road and where it ends, keep ahead along a track signposted to Glencallum Bay. In turn where this track ends, keep ahead through a kissing-gate and continue along a path. This superb coast path keeps below cliffs and above the shore, going through several kissing-gates and across boardwalks in places, following signs to Glencallum Bay. Approaching the bay, the path becomes increasingly rocky but, though faint at times, is generally discernible.

Keep to the right of the lighthouse to reach Glencallum Bay and, when in line with it, the path turns right **Ⓐ** to follow the curve of the bay. As you round the opposite (west) side, look out for a path on the right which heads steeply up the cliff to a green marker post. Turn left and for the rest of the walk you follow these posts – green with white arrows.

As the path continues, a magnificent view unfolds ahead along the rocky and indented south coast of Bute, with the mountains of Arran on the horizon. The path now bears slightly right away from the sea, contouring across the grassy hillside dotted with gorse, to reach another marker post **Ⓑ**. At this point turn right through a gap in the cliffs and, as you start to descend, the lovely, secretive-looking Loch na Leighe comes

SCALE 1:25 000 or 2½ INCHES to 1 MILE 4CM to 1KM

| 0 | 200 | 400 | 600 | 800 METRES | 1 |
| 0 | 200 | 400 | 600 YARDS | ½ |

KILOMETRES MILES

into sight. Keep along the base of a small hill to the left of the loch, bear right at a marker post to join a track and the track (likely to be muddy) which descends and continues through the valley towards Plan Farm.

Before reaching the farm, turn right over a plank footbridge, at a sign to St Blane's and Suidhe Chatain, keep ahead over another one and turn left alongside a small burn on the left to join a broad track. At the next footpath sign to St Blane's in front of a gate, bear right along a parallel path to a gate, go through and bear right uphill, making for the group of trees in front of which lies St Blane's Church.

Bear slightly left to go through a gate which admits you to the precincts of the church **C**, turn right and head up to the peaceful and atmospheric ruins, occupying an idyllic location on a secluded and tree-shaded knoll within an oval-shaped enclosure. The present church dates mainly from the 12th century and has a fine Norman chancel arch, but it stands on the site of a much earlier Celtic monastery, founded in the 6th century by St Blane, who was born

KILCHATTAN BAY, ST BLANE'S CHURCH AND SUIDHE CHATAIN ● 53

St Blane's Church

on the island. The remains of this monastery, destroyed during Viking raids, are scattered all over the site and include the foundations of buildings, tombs, crosses and a stone basin in which pilgrims used to wash their feet.

Continue past the church, go through a gap in the Vallum – a notice informs you that this marked the boundary of the Dark Age Celtic monastery – and walk along a path, passing the base of an ancient cross, to a gate. Go through the gate, turn left along a track, at a footpath sign to Suidhe Hill, and follow it as it winds steadily uphill to a marker post at the top. A few yards ahead the track ends at a stile. Climb it, turn right and head down into a dip. Go through a metal gate at the bottom, cross a burn and head uphill along the right edge of a field. Go through another gate and continue uphill, then turn right at a fence corner and keep ahead to the next gate **D**.

At this point you can turn left and head steeply up the grassy slopes to the summit of Suidhe Chatain, climbing a stile in a fence and over a low wall, to reach the triangulation pillar **E**. Despite a modest height of 515ft (157m), the extensive, all-round views are magnificent, taking in the Ayrshire coast, the Cowal and Kintyre peninsulas, the islands of Arran and Great and Little Cumbrae, and both coasts of Bute, with the lush, pastoral landscape of the interior of the island spread out below.

Return to the gate **D**, go through, bear left to a marker post and head downhill, bearing left again and making for the bottom left-hand corner of the field. Go through a kissing-gate, continue steeply downhill, by a wall bordering woodland on the left, climb a stile and keep ahead through trees down towards the houses of Kilchattan Bay. Just before reaching their gardens, turn left through a fence gap, keep ahead for a few yards and turn right along a track between houses to a road. Turn right to return to the start. ●

Barr and the Water of Gregg

Start	Changue car park, nearly 1 mile (1.6km) east of Barr village
Distance	6½ miles (10.5km)
Approximate time	3½ hours
Parking	Changue car park
Refreshments	Pub at Barr
Ordnance Survey maps	Landranger 76 (Girvan, Ballantrae & Barrhill), Outdoor Leisure 32 (Galloway Forest Park)

After a short walk beside the Water of Gregg into the village of Barr, you climb to a fine viewpoint on the edge of Carrick Forest overlooking the Stinchar valley. A descent into the valley is followed by an attractive walk beside another stretch of the Water of Gregg. Then comes a climb over forested slopes to descend to Changue Burn and the final part of the route contours along the side of the valley, giving more superb views. The climbs are all easy and gradual.

From the starting point in the car park turn left down a track to a T-junction and turn right alongside the Water of Gregg on the left. The track soon becomes a tarmac one and you follow it around a right bend and on into the attractive village of Barr, where the Water of Gregg flows into the River Stinchar.

Cross the second footbridge on the left **Ⓐ** – opposite Glenginnet Road – walk along a path across grass to a road and then turn left. The first part of the route follows green-waymarked posts. Where the road peters out, continue along an uphill track and turn right over a stile in front of a metal gate. Head uphill, making for the left

edge of a field, and at a fence corner ford a burn and climb a stile. Bear right along a track to climb another one, walk uphill and where the track

Barr Village

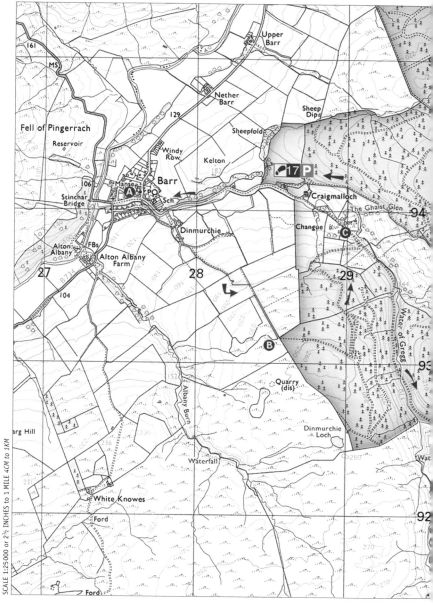

SCALE 1:25000 or 2½ INCHES to 1 MILE 4CM to 1KM

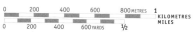

emerges on to open grassy moorland, bear right at a fork and continue uphill, by a wire fence on the right. At another fork in front of two gates, go through the left-hand gate but at the next fork immediately ahead take the right-hand track.

Pass to the left of a barn and continue uphill to climb a stile. Bear slightly right along an enclosed track – though the enclosing wall on the right has mostly disappeared – climb another stile just to the right of the track and head up towards the edge of the conifers of Changue Plantation, part of the vast Carrick Forest. Climb a stile, after a few yards turn left over a stone

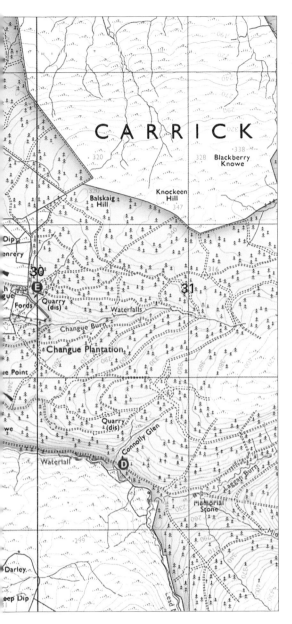

right **C** to keep above the Water of Gregg. For the remainder of the walk you follow purple waymarks. Cross the burn and continue above the other side of it as far as a 'Devil's Trail' sign. The name of this trail originates from a legend that near High Changue Farm is the site of a battle between a laird of Changue and the Devil, in which the laird came off best.

At the sign, turn left **D** along a path which bends sharp left and climbs through the conifers, later curving right to a T-junction. Turn left on to a track which first winds gently downhill and then ascends again, looking out for where a purple-waymarked post directs you to turn left down a grassy path. The path descends steeply to cross a footbridge over Changue Burn and climbs up the other side of the valley, curving left towards High Changue Farm.

At a waymarked post, turn right and then bear left up steps and through trees on to a track. Turn left **E** and follow the track as it contours along the side of the valley, giving a succession of fine views. At a fork keep ahead along the left-hand track which descends along the left edge of conifers – later by a line of impressive old beeches on the left – to return to the car park. ●

stile **B**, by a green-waymarked post, and continue along a broad track through the forest.

Descend gently to a T-junction and turn left along a track that winds downhill, initially still through the conifers but later across open country, with fine views over the Stinchar valley. Go through a gate, continue down and on meeting another track, turn sharp

Kildonan and Bennan Head

Start	Kildonan, car park at east end of village by a standing stone
Distance	6½ miles (10.5km)
Approximate time	3 hours
Parking	Kildonan
Refreshments	Hotels and tearoom at Kildonan
Ordnance Survey maps	Landranger 69 (Isle of Arran), Outdoor Leisure 37 (Isle of Arran)

This easy walk on the south coast of Arran takes you, via a combination of lane, foreshore path and beach, from the scattered and strung out hamlet of Kildonan to the Black Cave at Bennan Head. There is also the opportunity to visit the remains of Kildonan Castle, which, though sparse, occupy a fine clifftop position with views across to the tiny island of Pladda and the Ayrshire mainland. An added bonus is the likelihood of spotting seals, either swimming in the sea or basking on the rocks.

From the starting point at the car park descend the flight of steps to the sandy beach and turn right to walk along it. Where the lane runs parallel to the beach, make your way on to it at any convenient point and continue on to

where the lane turns right by a telephone box **Ⓐ**.

Keep ahead here along a track, passing in front of the village store and post office (also a tearoom) and then continue along a path, sometimes along

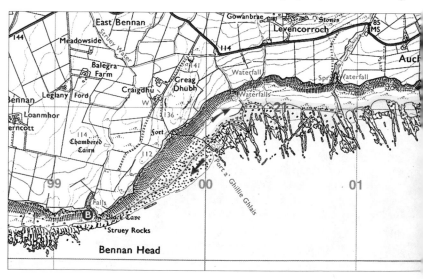

the edge of the foreshore and sometimes across the beach, towards the cliffs ahead. Walk along the base of the cliffs to Bennan Head and Black Cave, again either along the grassy foreshore – which may be muddy in places – or along the rocky beach. For the last stretch – after the path peters out – there is no alternative but to make your way carefully between boulders to the entrance to the cave **B**. Note that if the tide is fully in you will have to climb up just above the water level. Black Cave is the highest cave on Arran and is cut out of the smooth black rock.

Bennan Head from Kildonan

From here retrace your steps to Kildonan but after joining the lane **A**, continue along it uphill to the car park. For the short extra loop to Kildonan Castle, keep along the lane and where it bends left, bear right along a track **C**. Follow it round a right bend, then a left bend and then another right bend and, where it ends, go through a gate to the castle remains. Only a few crumbling walls of this medieval fortress have survived, but it makes an imposing sight and is a superb viewpoint.

Take the narrow grassy path to the right of the ruins which descends to the shore and turn right **D** first across a marshy area and then a few rocks to reach the fine sandy beach. Look out for the steps on the right which lead back up to the car park. ●

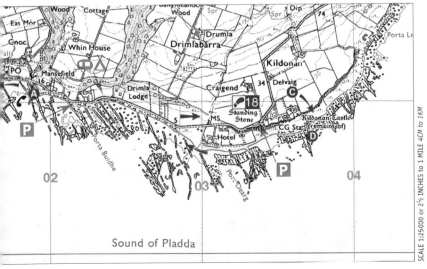

Kingarth and Dunagoil Fort

Start	Kingarth, at junction of A844 and minor road to St Blane's Church
Distance	7½ miles (12.1km) Shorter version 6 miles (9.7km)
Approximate time	3½ hours (2½ hours for shorter walk)
Parking	On verge beside road at Kingarth
Refreshments	Hotel at Kingarth, hotel at Kilchattan Bay
Ordnance Survey maps	Landranger 63 (Firth of Clyde), Pathfinder 428, NS 05/15 (The Cumbraes)

There is much scenic and historic appeal on this walk at the southern end of the Isle of Bute. It includes three sandy bays, imposing cliffs and attractive woodland, and the route passes two prehistoric sites. The shorter version omits the detour to Stravanan Bay.

The early-19th-century Kingarth Church used to stand at the road junction where the walk begins but this was demolished in 1968 following severe damage in a hurricane. Walk along the lane signposted to St Blane's Church, keeping along the right edge of a conifer plantation, and at a sign 'Stone Circle', turn left into a cleared area **A**. Just to the right are three standing stones, thought to have been part of a stone circle erected around 1500 BC.

Return to the lane and continue along it as it bends left and heads uphill after passing Largizean Farm, then bends right and, after Lubas Farm, keeps in a straight line. Just before the next farm – Dunagoil – turn right **B** through a metal gate and walk along a track towards Dunagoil Bay. Go through another metal gate and head across the grass to a wall corner where there is an information notice about Dunagoil Fort **C**.

This Iron Age fort, situated on top of the cliffs, was occupied from around

200 BC to 200 AD. At the seaward end some of the vitrified stones (i.e. stones fused by heat) that formed the core of the rampart can be seen. For a thorough exploration, you need to approach from the beach and a detailed guidebook is available from the tourist information centre in Rothesay. There is not a lot left to see and it is difficult for the layman to distinguish between the natural rock and the collapsed walls of the fort, but the site is an impressive one – even if a lot of imagination is required – and the views are splendid.

Retrace your steps back along the lane as far as footpath signs to Stravanan Bay on the left and Kilchattan Bay on the right **D**.

The shorter walk turns right here.

For the full walk that includes the detour to Stravanan Bay, turn left through a kissing-gate and walk along the left edge of a field. Cross a

0	200	400	600	800 METRES	1	
						KILOMETRES
						MILES
0	200	400	600 YARDS		½	

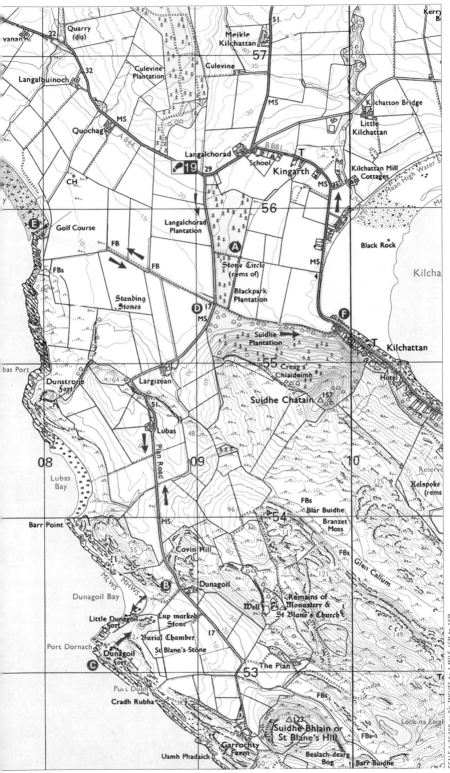

SCALE 1:25000 or 2½ INCHES to 1 MILE 4CM to 1KM

footbridge, keep along the left edge of the next two fields, climbing a stile, and in the corner of the second field, cross another footbridge and climb another stile. Keep ahead between gorse bushes across the corner of a golf course, then continue through more gorse and across soft, marshy ground, bearing right towards the far side. Here stiles admit you to the sandy, rocky beach of Stravanan Bay **E**.

Retrace your steps to the lane **D**, cross it – here rejoining the shorter walk – and take the track ahead signposted to Kilchattan Bay. The track – likely to be muddy – keeps mainly along the left inside edge of attractive birch and oak woodland and there are some fine views over Kilchattan Bay. At a fork, take the left-hand lower track and follow it down between houses on to the road at Kilchattan Bay **F**.

Turn right for the hotel; otherwise turn left along the road to a T-junction by the Kingarth Hotel. Turn left to return to the start.

Dunagoil Fort

Clauchlands Point and Dun Fionn

Start	Clauchlands, third (and last) car park on lane that runs along shore of Lamlash Bay to the north east of Lamlash near Kerr's Point
Distance	6 miles (9.7km)
Approximate time	3½ hours
Parking	Clauchlands
Refreshments	None
Ordnance Survey maps	Landranger 69 (Isle of Arran), Outdoor Leisure 37 (Isle of Arran)

From many points on this walk there are splendid views along the coast across Lamlash and Brodick Bays, and inland over the rolling, forested hills on the east side of Arran. The climb along the clifftop to Dun Fionn is steady rather than strenuous and this is followed by a descent, mainly through woodland and along tree-lined paths and tracks, to reach the shore. From here an easy and attractive, if at times muddy, coast path leads back to the start.

Begin by climbing the stile at the side of the car park and walk along a track beside the shore of Lamlash Bay to Clauchlands Point. The rock just off the point, Hamilton Isle, is usually crammed with sea birds, and you may well see seals on this part of the walk. After rounding the point, continue along a path to a combined stile and gate **Ⓐ**.

Climb it, turn left – a faint path is visible – and head steeply uphill to the top of the cliff. Follow the path – now much clearer – to the right and continue ascending along the clifftop, by a wire fence on the left. The path later climbs more steeply, levels off for a while and then climbs steeply again to reach the triangulation pillar on Dun Fionn **Ⓑ**, 540ft (164m) high and the site of an

Iron Age fort. The magnificent coastal views from here extend across Lamlash Bay to the prominent bulk of Holy Island, across Brodick Bay to Brodick Castle and the unmistakable Goatfell, and across the Firth of Clyde to the Cumbraes, Bute and the Ayrshire coast. The views of the forested slopes inland are also impressive.

Continue past the triangulation pillar to drop steeply into a hollow and climb again towards the edge of the forest. Do not climb the stile ahead into the forest but turn right and head quite steeply downhill, alongside the forest fence on the left, to a stile and gate. Climb it (or go through it), continue downhill through rather gloomy conifers, climb (or go through) another stile and gate, cross a small burn and the path

SCALE 1:25000 or 2½ INCHES to 1 MILE 4CM to 1KM

descends to a track just to the left of a farm **C**.

Turn left along this pleasant tree- and hedge-lined track and after a right bend, it becomes a tarmac lane. After ¼ mile (400m) and on reaching some houses, turn right **D** on to a track by a pillar box. Follow the track to Whitehill Farm where it bends to the right and continues gently downhill to the shore. Here it bends right again **E** beside the shore but shortly peters out in front of a wooden house.

Walk across a sandy and stony beach towards the trees ahead where you pick up a definite path again and continue along it across the grassy foreshore. The path is boggy and stony in places and you need to pick your way carefully. After climbing a stile, continue below steep cliffs and the path later contours along the side of the cliffs to reach the combined gate and stile climbed just after the start of the walk Ⓐ.

Here you pick up the outward route and retrace your steps to the starting point at the car park.

Holy Island from Clauchlands Point

Coire-Fhionn Lochan

Start	Thundergay, a small hamlet on the A841 between Catacol and Pirnmill
Distance	4 miles (6.4km)
Approximate time	2½ hours
Parking	Small parking spaces on the verge at Thundergay near public footpath sign to Coire Lochan
Refreshments	None
Ordnance Survey maps	Landranger 69 (Isle of Arran), Outdoor Leisure 37 (Isle of Arran)

A delightful climb along a path beside a burn, passing several attractive cascades, leads from the north-west coast of Arran to a beautiful, secluded, mysterious-looking lochan, cradled by bare hills. On the return descent the views across Kilbrannan Sound to Kintyre are superb, and in clear conditions extend to the Paps of Jura. The climb is steady and relatively easy but expect some wet conditions underfoot in places. There are also two burns to ford and one short, steep section across boulders where care is needed, particularly on the descent.

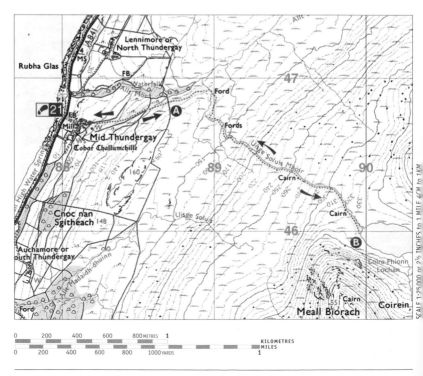

Approaching Coire-Fhionn Lochan

Begin by taking the track, at a public footpath sign to Coire Lochan, that heads uphill away from the shore. The track bends left, then turns right by the Arran Pottery, and turns left again between the few cottages that make up the hamlet of Thundergay. After another right turn, you reach two metal gates just beyond the last cottage.

Go through the right-hand gate and continue uphill, initially by a wire fence on the left but veering right away from it to join a clearer and more obvious path. The path heads up between bracken and heather to a ladder stile in a deer fence **A**. Climb it and now grand views open up ahead of heather- and bracken-clad hillsides.

After fording a burn, turn right and the path later veers left to continue in the direction of the prominent bulk of Meall Biorach. After fording another burn, the path now starts to ascend more steeply beside a burn on the left that tumbles down the hillside in a series of cascades. A steep rocky section beside a cascade follows and then comes a more gentle ascent. Finally the path levels off and continues beside the burn to Coire-Fhionn Lochan, a delightful spot **B**. The crystal clear waters of the lochan are framed on three sides by steep and bare hillsides and there is an appealing quality about the undoubtedly lonely, austere and even mysterious atmosphere that pervades.

From the lochan retrace your steps to the start, taking care on the steep, rocky part of the descent and enjoying the wonderful views across the water to Kintyre and Jura. ●

Craignethan Castle and the Clyde Valley

Start	Crossford
Distance	6½ miles (10.5km)
Approximate time	3½ hours
Parking	Crossford
Refreshments	Pub at Crossford
Ordnance Survey maps	Landrangers 64 (Glasgow, Motherwell & Airdrie) and 72 (Upper Clyde Valley, Biggar & Lanark), Pathfinders 445, NS 64/74 (Strathaven & District) and 446, NS 84/94 (Lanark)

Initially the route climbs along the western flanks of the Clyde Valley and then follows the track of a disused railway to the village of Netherburn. It continues along the disused railway track to Craignethan Castle, which occupies a dramatic position above the thickly-wooded Nethan Gorge. A descent along the side of the gorge brings you back into the Clyde Valley. There are some superb views over the valley and the climbing is steady rather than strenuous. One short section of path, just after leaving the road to the north of Crossford, is presently overgrown and rather difficult to negotiate; otherwise the walk presents no problems.

Turn right out of the car park through the village and follow the road above an attractive stretch of the River Clyde. After about ½ mile (800m) **A**, turn left on to a track in front of a house called Glenside and at a fork immediately in front take the right-hand track which heads uphill between houses.

Before reaching a gate, look out for a faint path leading off to the right. The next part of the walk is rather difficult as it is overgrown by trees and scrub, but as you make your way through there is a visible path in places, which keeps above a burn on the right, and after about 200 yds (183m) you reach a stile. After climbing the stile the conditions improve.

Keep ahead uphill along the right edge of a field, climb a stile and continue through gorse bushes to climb another one. Continue uphill, now along the left edge of a field, climb a stile in the top corner and turn left along an enclosed track. The track bends right and continues to a stile. Climb the stile, cross a road **B** and take the enclosed track opposite, at a public footpath sign 'North Netherburn, Langlea'. Follow this track, passing through a barrier at one stage, and then go through a metal gate on to a road.

Continue along it and at a public footpath sign to Hill Road turn left **C** on to a path which descends steps to cross a footbridge over a burn. Climb some steps, pass beside a barrier and walk along the left edge of a field.

Climb a stile in the field corner and turn left on to the track of a disused railway **D**. Follow this hedge-lined track to a road on the edge of Netherburn, keep

Clyde Valley near Crossford

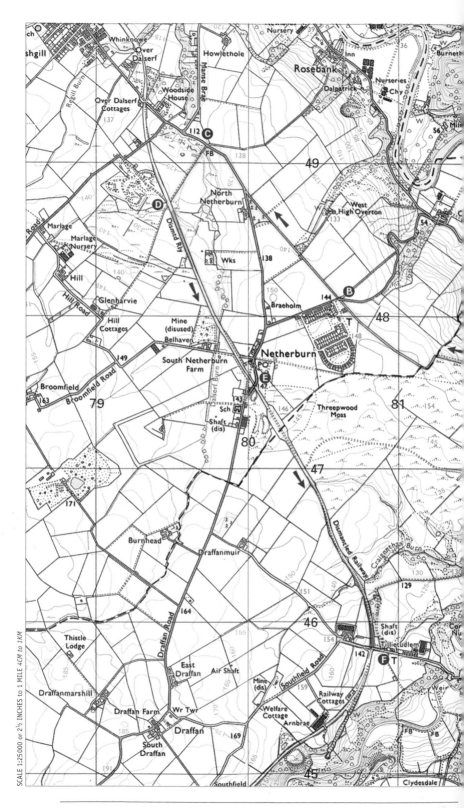

SCALE 1:25000 or 2½ INCHES to 1 MILE *4CM to 1KM*

ahead along the road which curves right to a junction and turn sharp left. Cross a bridge over the disused railway track **E**, turn sharp right and then descend beside the bridge to rejoin the disused track.

Continue along it for roughly 1½ miles (2.4km), climbing a stile in a fence at one stage, to reach an embankment where a road crosses the track on the edge of Tillietudlem. Turn left along the base of the embankment and, after a few yards, turn left on to a tarmac drive **F**. This is the drive to Craignethan Castle and you follow it around a right bend, go through a kissing-gate beside a cattle-grid and head downhill beside the castle. This imposing 16th-century fortress, a stronghold of the powerful Hamilton family, stands in a commanding position above the Nethan Gorge. It is almost certainly the model for 'Tillietudlem Castle' which features in Sir Walter Scott's historical novel *Old Mortality*.

As it descends, the drive turns first sharp right and then left. At a public footpath sign, turn left across grass to go through a kissing-gate, turn right down steps and continue down to cross a footbridge over a burn. Climb steps and, with a wire fence on the right, continue above the thickly-wooded Nethan Gorge, a Scottish Wildlife Trust Wildlife Reserve, to a stile. Climb the stile, keep ahead, now with the wire fence on the left, and the path descends along the side of the gorge – it is a long descent with steps at intervals – to eventually go through a squeezer stile on to a road on the edge of the village of Crossford.

Turn right over the River Nethan to return to the start. ●

Alloway and the Heads of Ayr

Start	Alloway, Burns' Cottage car park
Distance	10 miles (16.1km) Shorter version 2 miles (3.2km)
Approximate time	5 hours (1 hour for shorter walk)
Parking	Alloway
Refreshments	Hotel at Alloway, tearoom at Burns' Cottage, restaurant at the Tam o'Shanter Experience, pub at Doonfoot
Ordnance Survey maps	Landranger 70 (Ayr & Kilmarnock), Pathfinder 479, NS 21/31 (Dunure & Dalrymple)

SCALE 1:25000 or 2½ INCHES to 1 MILE 4CM to 1KM

The shorter walk is basically a Burns Trail around Alloway which begins near the cottage in which he was born and includes the Monument Gardens, Auld Brig o'Doon, Auld Kirk and a short walk by 'The banks and braes o'Bonnie Doon'. The full walk then continues to the mouth of the River Doon and proceeds along an attractive and unspoilt stretch of the Ayrshire coast, passing below the ruins of Greenan Castle, to the prominent cliffs of the Heads of Ayr. The return is by the same route. On the coastal section there are grand views across the Firth of Clyde to Arran.

From the car park a short distance to the left along the road brings you to the long, low, whitewashed thatched cottage in which Robert Burns was born on 25 January 1759. At the time of his birth Alloway was a tiny separate village but has now become a suburb of Ayr. Next to the cottage is a Burns Museum. Because of the proximity of so

Burns Monument, Alloway

steps to a road, turn left and then immediately turn right to cross the Auld Brig which spans the River Doon, a fine viewpoint **Ⓐ**. Take the path ahead which turns right to a road and turn right to re-cross the river, continuing to the ruined Alloway Auld Kirk. In the kirkyard is the grave of William Burns, the poet's father.

After passing the church take the first turning on the left **Ⓑ** – Shanter Way – and where the road ends, keep ahead along a track. Shortly turn left to descend steps and turn right to walk along a very attractive, tree-shaded riverside path. The path later climbs to rejoin the track which bears right and continues to a road **Ⓒ**.

If only attempting the short Burns Trail, turn right here to return to the car park.

For the full walk, turn left to a T-junction, turn left to cross the Doon again and turn right along Scaur o'Doon Road **Ⓓ**. Where the road bears left, keep ahead along a tarmac drive and through a car park to the mouth of the Doon.

Turn left **Ⓔ** on to a grassy path above the beach towards the meagre but dramatically-sited ruins of Greenan Castle, a former stronghold of the Kennedy clan, perched precariously on the cliff edge. The path joins the beach to pass below the castle and along the shore to the impressive cliffs of the Heads of Ayr. All the way there are grand views across the sea to the mountains of Arran. If the tide is in, turn back at this point but otherwise continue along the base of the cliffs to the beautiful Bracken Bay, an example of a raised beach about 25ft (7.6m) above shore level **Ⓕ**.

From here retrace your steps to where you left the short version of the walk **Ⓒ** and continue along the road to the starting point at the car park. ●

many places closely associated with Scotland's national poet, the area between here and the Auld Brig o'Doon has become a Burns National Heritage Park.

Return to the car park and just beyond it turn left on to a paved path, at a footpath sign to Auld Kirk and Auld Brig. The path initially runs parallel to the main road and then bends left to a road. Turn right, keep ahead across the car park of the Tam o'Shanter Experience, a visitor centre opened in 1995, following directions to Monument Gardens and Auld Brig, and at the far end join another paved path which bends right and then turns left to enter the beautifully maintained Burns Monument Gardens. The monument, overlooking the river and built in the style of a Greek temple, dates from 1823.

Walk through the gardens, descend

The Greenock Cut and Shielhill Glen

Start	Cornalees Bridge Visitor Centre, signposted from the A78 between Greenock and Largs
Distance	9 miles (14.5km)
Approximate time	4½ hours
Parking	Cornalees Bridge
Refreshments	Kiosk at the visitor centre
Ordnance Survey maps	Landranger 63 (Firth of Clyde), Pathfinder 402, NS 27/37 (Greenock & Port Glasgow)

After an initial walk across open moorland, most of the remainder of the route keeps beside the Greenock Cut, a channel constructed to transport water to Greenock, as it contours along the side of the hills above the Firth of Clyde. The extensive and constantly changing views over Greenock and the Clyde to Dunoon and the hills of Cowal, the Isle of Bute and the Cumbraes are outstanding. In contrast, the last part of the walk is through the beautiful, steep-sided, wooded Shielhill Glen.

Turn left out of the car park, go through a gate beside a cattle-grid and walk along a tarmac track beside the Compensation Reservoir for Loch Thom.

The track climbs gently to go through a kissing-gate by Loch Thom and continues – now as a rough track – steadily uphill across open moorland.

Greenock Cut

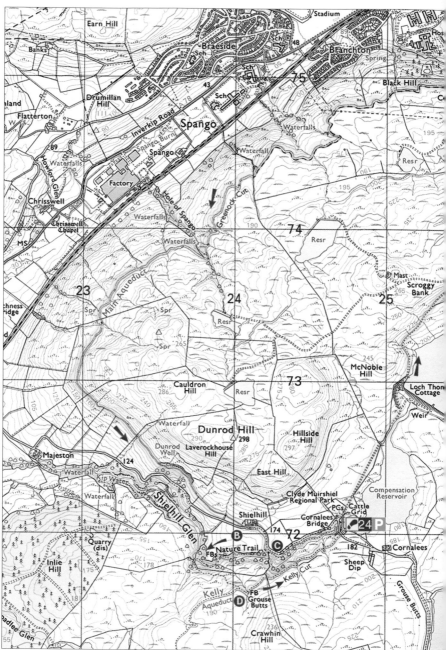

After going over a pass and starting to descend, views open up ahead across the Clyde to the southern rim of the Highlands, with Greenock immediately below.

Pass to the left of a small reservoir, turn right around the end of it and turn left, keeping to the left of another small reservoir. There are several metal kissing-gates on this part of the walk. After going through a kissing-gate beside the Waterman's Cottage at Overton, cross a bridge and turn left **A** on to the path that runs alongside the

engineer, to bring water from the reservoir which bears his name to Greenock. From Overton it cascaded down to the River Clyde, providing both drinking water to the town and power to the local industries.

The path keeps beside the Cut for nearly 4½ miles (7.2km) as it twists and turns, contouring along the hillside like a Madeiran levada, crossing several burns and lined by gorse bushes. There are more metal kissing-gates to go through and you pass a number of attractive stone bridges across the Cut. All the time there are superb views to the right across the Firth of Clyde to Dunoon and Cowal, later of Bute and the Cumbraes, with the buildings of Greenock below.

Finally the path emerges on to a lane by Shielhill Farm **B**. Cross over, go through a metal kissing-gate opposite and continue by the Cut for about another 300 yds (274m) to where it curves left towards the next kissing-gate. At this point turn sharp right down steps **C**, by a picnic area, go through a gate and follow a path gently downhill along the right edge of the wooded Shielhill Glen. The path curves left into the trees and bends right alongside the burn. Continue across a series of boardwalks and over a succession of footbridges, crossing and re-crossing the burn.

After turning left to cross the burn for the last time, the path reaches a kissing-gate. Go through and now you ascend a long flight of steps, emerging from the trees and climbing across heathery moorland, to a T-junction of paths in front of another cut **D**. This is the Kelly Cut, built in 1845 to supplement the Greenock Cut. Turn left and keep beside the Cut as it winds above Shielhill Glen – through more kissing-gates – to emerge on to a lane. Turn left to return to the start. ●

Greenock Cut. This remarkable piece of engineering, an aqueduct nearly 5 miles (8km) long, was constructed between 1825 and 1827 by Robert Thom, a civil

Ayr – Town, River and Valley

Start	Ayr
Distance	10½ miles (16.9km) Shorter version 4½ miles (7.2km)
Approximate time	5 hours (2 hours for the shorter walk)
Parking	Ayr
Refreshments	Pubs and cafés at Ayr
Ordnance Survey maps	Landranger 70 (Ayr & Kilmarnock), Pathfinder 455, NS 32/33 (Ayr, Prestwick & Troon)

The first and last parts of the route are pleasant riverside walks along the banks of the River Ayr, a 'green corridor' leading out into the countryside from the town centre of Ayr. The remainder of the walk takes you around the low hills on both sides of the valley, descending once to cross the river at Oswald's Bridge. Although the full walk is a lengthy one, there are only a few gradual climbs but these do give you extensive views across the valley. The shorter version is an easy 'up and down the river' stroll.

Ayr grew up as a port beside the mouth of the River Ayr and the oldest part of the town is near the river. Here is the 13th-century Auld Brig, Loudon Hall, a fine late-medieval townhouse, and the 17th-century Auld Kirk. In the mid-17th century, Oliver Cromwell, recognising the town's strategic importance, built a citadel, some of the walls of which can still be seen on the south side of the harbour. Fine sandy beaches and easy access to industrial Clydeside enabled Ayr to develop into a seaside resort in the 19th century and some elegant Victorian terraces survive from that era.

The walk begins in front of the imposing 19th-century Town Hall. Facing it, walk along the street to the left of it (High Street) and take the first

turning on the left to cross the Auld Brig across the River Ayr. Turn right along River Terrace and where the road ends, keep ahead along a paved riverside path. After passing under a road bridge, the path continues first beside a sports stadium, then along the edge of an attractive park, passing a footbridge , and later alongside a golf course. The path forks twice; on both occasions take the right-hand path to keep beside the river all the way up to the main A77 .

If doing the short walk, turn right over Overmills Bridge and turn right down steps to join a path on the other side of the river.

For the full walk, turn left along the road and take the first turning on the right, signposted Mainholm Smallholdings. Follow the lane around a right bend, then take the first turning on the left and keep along this quiet and narrow lane for nearly $1\frac{1}{2}$ miles (2.4km) to where it becomes a rough track. The track continues through a metal gate, heads uphill into woodland

and bends left to reach a fork. Take the right-hand upper path which first bends right and then curves left up through Newbarns Wood to a gate and stile. Climb the stile and turn right along a straight, wide track. Oswald's Tower, the monument now seen in front, is thought to have been a former tea house belonging to the Auchincruive estate. The estate belonged to the Oswald family but now forms the West of Scotland Agricultural College. Go through a gate and follow the track gently downhill to a road .

Turn right and the road descends to cross the River Ayr at Oswald's Bridge, a most attractive spot. It then bends right through Laigland (or Leglen) Wood and you keep along it for $\frac{3}{4}$ mile (1.2km) before taking the second turning on the right , beside a farm and opposite a bungalow called The Croft. Walk along a track, passing through a series of metal gates, head uphill towards woodland and the track curves right to

Ayr Valley, near Ayr

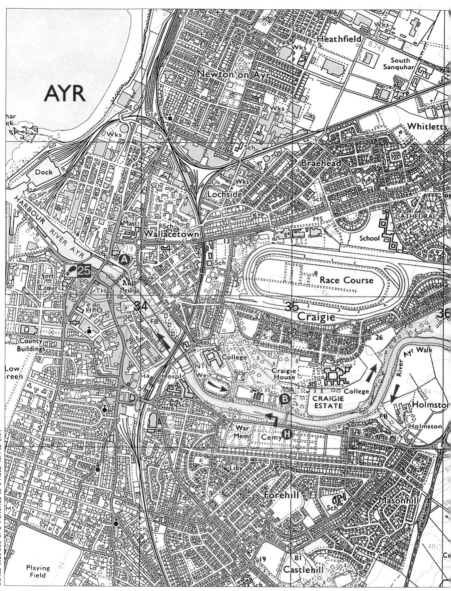

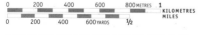

keep along the right edge of the trees. From here there are fine views to the right over the valley to Ayr and the coast, with the cliffs of the Heads of Ayr and the mountains of Arran clearly visible.

Go through a metal gate and the track later turns right, still keeping by the edge of the wood, and continues in a straight line, passing through a series of gates, to reach Gateside Farm. Keep to the left of the farm and head gently downhill along a tarmac track to a road. Turn right, take the first turning on the right ⓖ to walk along a tarmac, hedge-lined drive and where this bends right to an electricity substation, keep ahead across grass, by a hedge and line of trees on the left.

Just before reaching the field corner, turn left through a gap in the hedge into woodland and at a fork take the right-hand path which winds downhill through the trees to emerge into a clearing. Keep ahead to a T junction of paths, turn right down to the River Ayr and the path turns left to pass under Overmills Bridge, here rejoining the short walk.

Continue along the riverside path and shortly after passing a plaque that commemorates the opening of the River Ayr Walk in 1910, the path rises and runs parallel to a road on the left. At a fork above a footbridge **H**, take the right-hand path to descend steps, turn sharp right and then turn left to cross the footbridge. Turn left **B**, here rejoining the outward route, and retrace your steps to the starting point at Ayr Town Hall.

●

Tinto Hill

Start	Car park just beyond Fallburn Farm, off A73 to the south-east of Lanark opposite road to Thankerton
Distance	4½ miles (7.2km)
Approximate time	2½ hours
Parking	Near Fallburn Farm
Refreshments	Café about 200 yds (183m) from the start
Ordnance Survey maps	Landranger 72 (Upper Clyde Valley, Biggar & Lanark), Pathfinder 458, NS 83/93 (Douglas & Symington)

The familiar landmark of Tinto Hill rises to 2334ft (711m) above the Clyde Valley and from both its slopes and summit, the views over the valley and the surrounding hills more than compensate for the effort expended in climbing it. In fact it is a relatively easy hill to climb as it is a steady rather than steep and strenuous ascent, with a good, clear path all the way up, and is well within the capabilities of most walkers. Because of its exposed position, it is best to avoid it in windy weather.

From the car park, the clear path can be seen heading up across the smooth grassy slopes of the hill towards the summit. Begin the walk by going through a kissing-gate and walking along a path, between wire fences, to another kissing-gate, signposted to Tinto Hill. Go through that kissing-gate, continue between wire fences and the path then rises gently to go through a final kissing-gate.

Now follow the path up to the summit. It soon starts to ascend more steeply but this is a steady (if unremitting) rather than a strenuous climb. After passing a cairn **Ⓐ**, there is

Tinto Hill

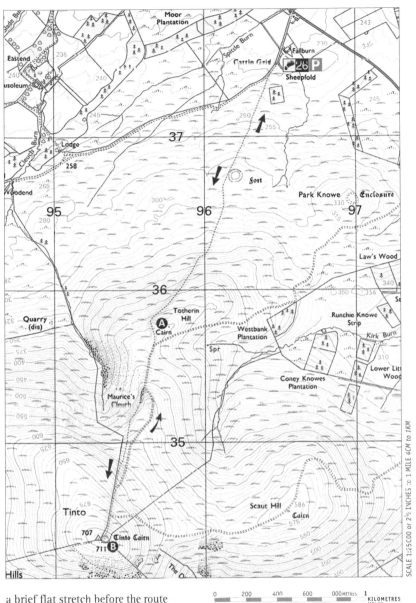

SCALE 1:25C00 or 2½ INCHES :c 1 MILE 4CM to 1KM

0	200	400	600	800 METRES	1
					KILOMETRES
					MILES
0	200	400	600 YARDS	½	

a brief flat stretch before the route now a broad track – rises again. At a fork, it does not matter if you take the path slightly to the right or bear left still on the wider track as they meet up again before the final pull up to the summit cairn **B**.

At the cairn – the triangulation pillar is just over a fence – a view indicator shows all the landmarks that can be seen from this magnificent all-round viewpoint. These include the Clyde Valley, the long line of the Southern Uplands, Merrick and many of the other Galloway hills, and in exceptionally clear conditions they extend to the southern edge of the Highlands, the hills of Cowal and Goatfell on the Isle of Arran.

Retrace your steps to the starting point, enjoying more superb views of the Clyde Valley spread out below as you descend.

●

Coast of North Arran

Start	South Newton, on east shore of Loch Ranza opposite Lochranza Castle
Distance	7½ miles (12.1km)
Approximate time	4½ hours
Parking	Parking areas on shore of Loch Ranza
Refreshments	None
Ordnance Survey maps	Landranger 69 (Isle of Arran), Outdoor Leisure 37 (Isle of Arran)

This superb walk is well worth taking plenty of time over and waiting for a fine day on which to do it. From the shores of Loch Ranza, the route climbs along the side of Glen Chalmadale and continues over the hills to reach a magnificent viewpoint overlooking the Sound of Bute. Then it gradually descends to the

coast at Laggan Cottage and the remainder of the walk keeps along the base of cliffs as it follows the shoreline around the northern tip of Arran to return to Loch Ranza. Parts of the coast path are likely to be muddy and marshy and there are some awkward rocky stretches to negotiate where both care and patience are required.

From the parking area there is a fine view across the loch to the mainly 13th- and 14th-century ruins of Lochranza Castle. Robert the Bruce is said to have landed here in 1307 from Ireland at the start of his campaign for Scottish independence. Begin by walking back down the lane and where it turns right, keep ahead **A** along a track, at a public footpath sign to Cock of Arran and Laggan. The track climbs steadily along the side of Glen Chalmadale and where

it levels off just before a cottage, take the grassy path to the left **B**, also signed to 'The Cock and Laggan'.

Continue ascending between bracken, crossing a footbridge, and at the top there is a boggy area to cross before picking up a clear and well-surfaced path again. At the top of this pass in the hills there are grand views over the

0	200	400	600	800 METRES	1	
						KILOMETRES
						MILES
0	200	400	600 YARDS		½	

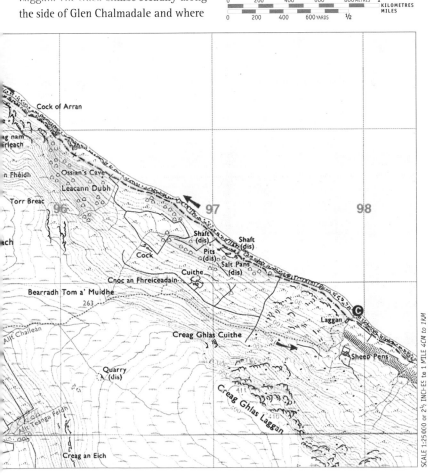

SCALE 1:25000 or 2½ INCHES to 1 MILE 4CN to 1KM

North Arran Coast

coast, looking across the Sound of Bute to the distant hills of the mainland. The path now gradually descends, contouring along the side of the hill and keeping roughly parallel to the coast below. Later it descends more steeply, turns left, swings left again and turns right to continue down to reach the shore to the left of Laggan Cottage **C**.

Turn left on to the coast path and follow it back to the start, keeping below cliffs all the way. On approaching a small wooded area, keep to the right of it, picking your way between boulders to reach some ruined buildings and the site of Laggan Harbour. It is difficult to believe that from this remote and tranquil spot coal used to be shipped, obtained from a thin local seam. Some of the pools that can be seen near the path are the old mine shafts.

Now comes an easier section along a glorious stretch of coast with some very impressive and unusual rock formations of smooth red sandstone. The huge sandstone boulder that is passed is known as the Cock of Arran, once a landmark for fishermen but now less impressive without its top layer. This is followed by the most difficult part of the route where you have to pick your way across a pile of boulders, the result of an 18th-century rock fall. Take your time and be careful. An easier alternative, if the tide is out, is to walk along the stony beach.

The route continues along the shore to the cottage at Fairy Dell **D**, backed by attractive woodland, and soon afterwards the houses of Lochranza come into sight on the far side of the loch. There are more marshy areas to cross before the path bears left around Newton Point to join a lane and return to the start. ●

Goatfell

Start	Brodick Castle Country Park. Alternative starting point for those not wishing to visit the country park is the Cladach car park on the A841
Distance	7 miles (11.3km)
Approximate time	6 hours
Parking	Brodick Castle Country Park or Cladach
Refreshments	Café at Brodick Castle
Ordnance Survey maps	Landranger 69 (Isle of Arran), Outdoor Leisure 37 (Isle of Arran)

At 2866ft (874m), Goatfell is both the highest point and the most familiar landmark on Arran, and the ascent of it from the south is probably the most popular walk on the island. For much of the way the route – initially through trees, bracken and heather and later across open, rocky hillside – is clearly defined and the climb is steady, though unremitting, rather than strenuous. However the final stretch is a steep and quite challenging scramble over boulders which requires stamina and some degree of fitness. Inevitably the views from the summit are magnificent and wide ranging on clear days. On no account should this walk be attempted in bad weather, especially in mist or wintry conditions, unless experienced and equipped for such conditions and able to navigate by using a compass.

The imposing, orange-coloured sandstone walls of Brodick Castle can be seen across the bay by visitors arriving on the ferry from Ardrossan. The castle, which dates back to the 13th century but was substantially enlarged in the 17th century and again in the 19th century, was the holiday home of the dukes of Hamilton and contains some fine furniture and collections of porcelain, silver and paintings. Now it is maintained by the National Trust for Scotland and its wooded grounds and colourful gardens make an attractive country park.

The main walk starts on the terrace in front of the castle from where there is a fine view across the bay to Brodick. Facing the sea, turn right and follow the gravel path round to the right, by the castle, to a T-junction. Turn left along a tarmac drive, go through a metal gate beside a cattle-grid and continue along to where a path crosses the drive **Ⓐ**. Turn right to begin the ascent of Goatfell.

If starting from the car park at Cladach, cross the road and take the track opposite, signposted Goatfell, which bears left, between the buildings of Arran Craft Centre on the left and Cladach Sawmill on the right. Turn right on to a path, at a Goatfell sign, which bears left uphill and then bends

On the ascent of Goatfell

right to reach a tarmac drive.  **A** *Keep ahead to join the main walk.*

The well-signposted path winds up-hill between conifers and continues between bracken, heather and trees above the steep, narrow valley of Cnocan Burn on the left. Shortly after turning right to cross a footbridge over a burn, the path reaches a gate in a wire fence **B**.

Go through and continue more steeply uphill across the open hillside along an increasingly rocky path marked by cairns. The abrupt summit cone of Goatfell is in sight for most of the way and there are fine views of the serrated ridges of the adjacent peaks. After turning left, there comes the steep, tiring final ascent, scrambling across boulders to eventually reach the triangulation pillar on the summit **C**. The all-round views from here are tremendous and a viewfinder helps you identify the vast range of places that can be seen on a clear day. They stretch to some of the peaks of Galloway and the Southern Uplands, the Cumbraes and the Isle of Bute, the hills of Cowal and the southern fringes of the Highlands, the long line of the Kintyre peninsula and the Paps of Jura.

Return by the same route, taking particular care on the first part of the descent and enjoying the grand views ahead over Brodick Bay, the east coast of Arran and across the Firth of Clyde to the Ayrshire coast. ●

Further Information

The Law and Tradition as they affect Walking in Scotland

The Law and Tradition as they affect Walking in Scotland

Walkers following the routes given in this book should not run into problems, but it is as well to know something about the law as it affects access, and also something of the traditions which can be quite different in Scotland from elsewhere in Britain. Most of this is common sense, observing the country code and having consideration for other people and their activities which, after all, may be their livelihood.

It is often said that there is no law of trespass in Scotland. In fact there is, but the trespass itself is not usually a criminal offence. You can be asked to leave any property, and technically 'reasonable force' may be used to obtain your compliance – though the term is not defined! You can be charged with causing damage due to the trespass, but this would be hard to establish if you were just walking on open, wild, hilly country where, whatever the law, in practice there has been a long tradition of free access for recreational walking – something both the Scottish Landowners' Federation and the Mountaineering Council of Scotland do not want to see changed.

There are certain restrictions. Walkers should obey the country code and seasonal restrictions arising from lambing or stalking. Where there is any likelihood of such restrictions this is mentioned in the text and visitors are asked to comply. When camping, use a campsite. Camp fires should not be lit; they are a danger to moorland and forest, and really not necessary as lightweight and efficient stoves are now available.

Many of the walks in this book are on rights of way. The watchdog on rights of way in Scotland is the Scottish Rights of Way Society (SRWS), who maintain details on all established cases and will, if

Castle Semple Loch

need be, contest attempted closures. They produce a booklet on the Scottish legal position (Rights of Way, A Guide to the Law in Scotland, 1991), and their green signposts are a familiar sight by many footpaths and tracks, indicating the lines of historic routes.

In Scotland rights of way are not marked on Ordnance Survey maps as is the case south of the border. It was not felt necessary to show these as such on the maps – a further reflection of the freedom to roam that is enjoyed in Scotland. So a path on a map is no indication of a right of way, and many paths and tracks of great use to walkers were built by estates as stalking paths or for private access. While you may traverse such paths, taking due care to avoid damage to property and the natural environment, you should obey restricted access notices and leave if asked to do so.

The only established rights of way are those where a court case has resulted in a legal judgment, but there are thousands of other 'claimed' rights of way. Local planning authorities have a duty to protect rights of way – no easy task with limited resources. Many attempts at closing claimed rights of way have been successfully contested in the courts by the Scottish Rights of Way Society and local authorities.

A dog on a lead or under control may also be taken on a right of way. There is little chance of meeting a free-range solitary bull on any of the walks. Any herds seen are not likely to be dairy cattle, but all cows can be inquisitive and may approach walkers, especially if they have a dog. Dogs running among stock may be shot on the spot; this is not draconian legislation but a desperate attempt to stop sheep and lambs being harmed, driven to panic or lost, sometimes with fatal results. Any practical points or restrictions applicable will be made in the text. If there is no comment it can be assumed that the route carries no real restrictions.

Scotland in fact likes to keep everything as natural as possible, so, for instance, waymarking is kept to a minimum (the Scottish Rights of Way Society signposts and Forest Walk markers are in unobtrusive colours). In Scotland people are asked to 'walk softly in the wilderness, to take nothing except photographs, and leave nothing except footprints' – which is better than any law.

Scotland's Hills and Mountains: a Concordat on Access

This remarkable agreement was published early in 1996 and is likely to have considerable influence on walkers' rights in Scotland in the future. The signatories include organisations which have formerly been at odds – the Scottish Landowners' Federation and the Ramblers' Association, for example. However they joined with others to make the Access Forum (a full list of signatories is detailed below). The RSPB and the National Trust for Scotland did not sign the Concordat initially but it is hoped that they will support its principles.

The signatories of the Concordat are:

Association of Deer Management Groups
Convention of Scottish Local Authorities
Mountaineering Council of Scotland
National Farmers' Union of Scotland
Ramblers' Association Scotland
Scottish Countryside Activities Council
Scottish Landowners' Federation
Scottish Natural Heritage
Scottish Sports Association
Scottish Sports Council

They agreed that the basis of access to the hills for the purposes of informal recreation should be:

Freedom of access exercised with responsibility and subject to reasonable constraints for management and conservation purposes.

Acceptance by visitors of the needs of land management, and understanding of how this sustains the livelihood, culture and community interests of those who live and work in the hills.

Acceptance by land managers of the public's expectation of having access to the hills.

Acknowledgment of a common interest in the natural beauty and special qualities of Scotland's hills, and the need to work together for their protection and enhancement.

The Forum point out that the success of the Concordat will depend on all who manage or visit the hills acting on these four principles. In addition, the parties to the Concordat will promote good practice in the form of:

- Courtesy and consideration at a personal level.

- A welcome to visitors.

Glossary of Gaelic Names

Most of the place-names in this region are Gaelic in origin, and this list gives some of the more common elements, which will allow readers to understand otherwise meaningless words and appreciate the relationship between place-names and landscape features. Place-names often have variant spellings, and the more common of these are given here.

aber	mouth of loch, river	eilidh	hind
abhainn	river	eòin, eun	bird
allt	stream	fionn	white
auch, ach	field	fraoch	heather
bal, bail, baile	town, homestead	gabhar, ghabhar,	
bàn	white, fair, pale	gobhar	goat
bealach	hill pass	garbh	rough
beg, beag	small	geal	white
ben, beinn	hill	ghlas, glas	grey
bhuidhe	yellow	gleann, glen	narrow, valley
blar	plain	gorm	blue, green
brae, braigh	upper slope, steepening	inbhir, inver	confluence
		inch, inis, innis	island, meadow by river
breac	speckled		
cairn	pile of stones, often marking a summit	lag, laggan	hollow
		làrach	old site
cam	crooked	làirig	pass
càrn	cairn, cairn-shaped hill	leac	slab
		liath	grey
caol, kyle	strait	loch	lake
ceann, ken, kin	head	lochan	small loch
cil, kil	church, cell	màm	pass, rise
clach	stone	maol	bald-shaped top
clachan	small village	monadh	upland, moor
cnoc	hill, knoll, knock	mór, mor(e)	big
coille, killie	wood	odhar, odhair	dun-coloured
corrie, coire,		rhu, rubha	point
choire	mountain hollow	ruadh	red, brown
craig, creag	cliff, crag	sgòr, sgòrr,	
crannog,		sgùrr	pointed
crannag	man-made island	sron	nose
dàl, dail	field, flat	stob	pointed
damh	stag	strath	valley (broader than glen)
dearg	red		
druim, drum	long ridge	tarsuinn	traverse, across
dubh, dhu	black, dark	tom	hillock (rounded)
dùn	hill fort	tòrr	hillock (more rugged)
eas	waterfall	tulloch, tulach	knoll
eilean	island	uisge	water, river

- Making advice readily available on the ground or in advance.
- Better information about the uplands and hill land uses through environmental education.
- Respect by visitors for the welfare needs of livestock and wildlife.
- Adherence to relevant codes and standards of good practice by visitors and land managers alike.
- Any local restrictions on access should be essential for the needs of management, should be fully explained, and be for the minimum period and area required.

Queries should be addressed to:
Access Forum Secretariat, c/o Recreation and Access Branch,
Scottish Natural Heritage, 2 Anderson Place, Edinburgh EH6 5NP.

Barr Village and the Stinchar valley

Safety on the Hills

The hills and lower but remote areas call for care and respect. The idyllic landscape of the tourist brochures can change rapidly into a world of gales, rain and mist, potentially lethal for those ill-equipped or lacking navigational skills. The Scottish hills in winter can be arctic in severity, and even in summer, snow can lash the summits.

At the very least carry adequate wind- and waterproof outer garments, food and drink to spare, a basic first-aid kit, whistle, map and compass – and know how to use them. Wear boots. Plan within your capabilities. If going alone ensure you leave details of your proposed route. Heed local advice, listen to weather forecasts, and do not hesitate to modify plans if conditions deteriorate.

Some of the walks in this book venture into remote country and others climb high summits, and these expeditions should

only be undertaken in good summer conditions. In winter they could well need the skills and experience of mountaineering rather than walking. In midwinter the hours of daylight are of course much curtailed, but given crisp, clear late-winter days many of the shorter expeditions would be perfectly feasible, if the guidelines given are adhered to.

Mountain Rescue

In case of emergency the standard procedure is to dial 999 and ask for the police who will assess and deal with the situation.

First, however, render first aid as required and make sure the casualty is made warm and comfortable. The distress signal (six flashes/whistle-blasts, repeated at minute intervals) may bring help from other walkers in the area. Write down essential details: exact location (six-figure reference), time of accident, numbers involved, details of injuries, steps already taken; then despatch a messenger to phone the police.

The rugged coast near Culzean Castle

If leaving the casualty alone, mark the site with an eye-catching object. Be patient; waiting for help can seem interminable.

Useful Organisations

Association for the Protection of Rural Scotland
Gladstone's Land, 3rd floor, 483 Lawnmarket, Edinburgh EH1 2NT
Tel. 0131 225 7012

Forestry Commission
Information Department, 231 Corstorphine Road, Edinburgh EH12 7AT
Tel. 0131 334 0303

Historic Scotland
Longmore House, Salisbury Place, Edinburgh EH9 1SH
Tel. 0131 668 8600

Long Distance Walkers' Association
21 Upcroft, Windsor, Berkshire SL4 3NH
Tel. 01753 866685

National Trust for Scotland
5 Charlotte Square, Edinburgh EH2 4DU
Tel. 0131 226 5922

Ordnance Survey
Romsey Road, Southampton SO16 4GU
Tel. 08456 05 05 05 (Lo-call)

Ramblers' Association (main office)
1/5 Wandsworth Road, London SW8 2XX
Tel. 0171 582 6878

Ramblers' Association (Scotland)
Kingfisher House, Auld Mart Business
Park, Milnathort, Kinross KY13 9DA
Tel. 01577 861222

Royal Society for the Protection of Bird
Abernethy Forest Reserve, Forest Lodge,
Nethybridge, Inverness-shire PH25 3EF
Tel. 01479 821409

Scottish Landowners' Federation
25 Maritime Street, Edinburgh EH6 5PW
Tel. 0131 555 1031

Scottish Natural Heritage
12 Hope Terrace, Edinburgh EH9 2AS
Tel. 0131447 4784

Scottish Rights of Way Society Ltd
John Cotton Business Centre,
10 Sunnyside, Edinburgh EH7 5RA
Tel. 0131 652 2937

Scottish Wildlife Trust
Cramond House, Kirk Cramond, Cramond
Glebe Road, Edinburgh EH4 6NS
Tel. 0131 312 7765

Scottish Youth Hostels Association
7 Glebe Crescent, Stirling FK8 2JA
Tel. 01786 891400

Tourist Information

Scottish Tourist Board
23 Ravelston Terrace, Edinburgh EH43EU
Tel. 0131 332 2433

Ayrshire and Arran Tourist Board
Burns House, Burns Statue Square, Ayr
KA7 1UT
Tel. 01292 288688

Greater Glasgow and Clyde Valley
Tourist Board
11 George Square, Glasgow G2 1DY
Tel. 0141 204 4400

Local tourist information offices:
Ayr 01292 288688
Brodick: 01770 302140/302401
Glasgow: 0141 204 4400
Glasgow Airport: 0141 848 4440
Greenock: 01475 722007

Hamilton: 01698 285590
Irvine: 01294 313886
Lanark: 01555 661661
Largs: 01475 673765
Millport: 01475 530753 (open Easter to
October)
Rothesay: 01700 502151

Weather Forecasts

Scotland seven-day forecast
Tel. 0891 112260
UK seven-day forecast Tel 0891 333123

Ordnance Survey Maps of Glasgow, the Clyde Valley, Ayrshire and Arran

The area of this title is covered by
Ordnance Survey 1:50 000 scale (1 1/4
inches to 1 mile or 2 cm to 1km)
Landranger map sheets 63, 64, 69, 70, 71,
72, 76, 77. These all-purpose maps are
packed with information to help you
explore the area and show viewpoints,
picnic sites, places of interest and caravan
and camping sites.

To examine the area in more detail and
especially if you are planning walks,
Ordnance Survey Outdoor Leisure maps
32, 37 at 1:25 000 (2 1/2 inches to 1 mile
or 4cm to 1km) scale are ideal.

The following Pathfinder maps also at
1:25,000 scale cover the area:

400 NR87/97	445 NS 64/74
402 NS27/37	446 NS84/94
403 NS47/57	455 NS32/33
414 NS06/16	458 NS83/93
415 NS26/36	479 NS 21/31
428 NS05/15	491 NS20/30
429 NS25/35	502 NX 29/39
431 NS65/75	

To get to this area use the Ordnance
Survey Great Britain Routeplanner Map
(Travelmaster map number 1) at 1:625 000
(1 inch to 10 miles or 1cm to 6.25 km)
scale or

Travelmaster map 4 (Southern Scotland
and Northumberland) at 1:250 000 (1
inch to 4 miles or 1cm to 2.5km) scale.

Ordnance Survey maps and guides are
available from most booksellers, stationers
and newsagents.

Index

Entries in *italic type* refer to illustrations